Standing Out

The Necessity of Admirable Character In A World Facing Moral Erosion.

Guidance For My Young Daughter.

by

Robert N. Jacobs

Grosvenor House
Publishing Limited

This book is published by
Grosvenor House Publishing Ltd
Link House
140 The Broadway, Tolworth, Surrey, KT6 7HT.
www.grosvenorhousepublishing.co.uk

A CIP record for this book
is available from the British Library

ISBN 978-1-80381-742-2
eBook ISBN 978-1-80381-772-9

Acknowledgements

To my dearest daughter, Ava!

This book, *Standing Out: The Necessity of Admirable Character in a World Facing Moral Erosion*, is, first and foremost, a letter to you. Your inquisitive spirit, your ever-present joy, and your uncanny ability to see the world with eyes wide open have been the wellspring of inspiration behind every line I have penned.

I remember a cold winter evening, when you were barely four, you asked me why it was important to be nice when people around us weren't always so. That innocent question lingered in my mind and eventually germinated into the idea of this book.

I am profoundly grateful to your mother, my rock, who has stood by my side, providing unwavering support in all my mad ventures. Her belief in me, even during times when my own resolve wavered, has been the wind beneath my wings.

My heartfelt thanks also go out to my parents, who taught me the significance of moral courage from a young age. Their lessons have shaped me and this book in ways too profound to articulate.

And to you, dear readers, I hope this book serves as a reminder of the pivotal role character plays in our personal lives and in the larger fabric of society.

But, most importantly, to you, my precious Ava, the heart of this book. My deepest desire is that you carry these lessons with you as you traverse the path of life. Remember, my *popolotti,* that in a world where you can be anything; be kind, be brave, and stand out by staying true to who you are.

May this book guide you as a compass, leading you to become a beacon of light in a world that is often shadowed by moral erosion.

With all the love my heart can hold,

Pappa

Foreword

As I pen down these words, an unforgettable quote by Mahatma Gandhi reverberates in my mind: "Be the change you want to see in the world". It is a powerful call to action that resonates deeply with the essence of this book, *Standing Out: The Necessity of Admirable Character in a World Facing Moral Erosion. Guidance for my Young Daughter.*

We live in a time where ethical ambiguity seems to be the norm rather than the exception. It's a world where moral erosion is gradually chipping away at the very foundations of our society. This book is not just a poignant narration of this decline, but also a beacon of hope, showing a path towards reestablishing a world guided by moral compasses.

The need for admirable character has never been more pronounced. In a society where integrity often takes a backseat to expediency, it is up to us, the individuals, to step forward and embody the virtues we wish to see around us. Just as a single candle can illuminate a room enveloped in darkness, so too can one person's moral fortitude shine a light on the path to righteousness for others.

Every chapter of this book serves as a stepping stone on the journey towards building an admirable character. They offer practical guidance and illustrate how living a morally upright life is not a burden, but rather a source of immense strength and inner peace.

Martin Luther King Jr. once said, "The time is always right to do what is right". This book is an earnest attempt to equip you, the reader, with the tools required to do just that. It encourages you to take charge of your moral standing, inspiring you to lead a life of integrity, kindness, and respect for others.

Living a life of moral uprightness is not only beneficial for oneself but is also a gift to society. It serves as an example for others, fostering a culture of honesty, empathy, and respect. It's about standing out, not just for personal advancement but for the betterment of our world.

To wrap up, this book goes beyond being a mere guide. It's a passionate call for all of us to hold ourselves accountable, to consider the impact of our actions, and to work towards a world where moral values are not just words on a page, but an integral part of our daily lives. While not religious in nature, I do explore the impact of faith in Chapter 9. I understand that this chapter may not be for everyone, and if that's the case, feel free to skip it. However, in our pursuit of knowledge, it may still be worth a read.

This book is an invitation for you to embark on a journey of self-discovery and growth. As you turn these pages, let them inspire you, challenge you, and ultimately guide you towards becoming the change you wish to see in the world.

Welcome to a journey of transformation. Welcome to a story of hope. Welcome to a life of admirable character.

Robert N. Jacobs
Advocate for Humanity

Contents

Chapter 1

Standing Out for the Right Reasons

The words "standing out" are often followed by "from the crowd". You could stand out by simply dying your hair an unusual colour or dressing in an avant-garde style, but standing out for the right reasons is nothing to do with how you look or appear, it's all about who you are and how you present yourself in what you do.

In your career, and in life, standing out for the right reasons is giving your best in all you do. Standing out is being memorable, and when it's for the right reasons, you are memorable in a good way, meaning you make and leave a good impression wherever you go. First impressions count, so whether you're going for a job interview or you're on a first date, creating a good impression can mean the difference between getting a second interview (or date) or not!

In all aspects of life, the way you present yourself and the way you behave become the impression you make on others. That impression then becomes associated with your name. The amazing thing about a "good name" or a "bad name" is that the impression you make on one person can become your reputation – and your reputation may go before you, even among people who have never met you in person.

A Good Name

Establishing a good name for yourself is a key element of standing out for the right reasons. Your name is your most valuable asset. It represents who you are, what you stand for, and how you approach life. Your name is your reputation, and as such it speaks volumes about what you do and how you do it.

Of course, your reputation reflects the way other people see you, so it's not something you have direct control over. However, you have the power to influence your reputation by taking full responsibility for your every thought, word, and action. In other words, everything you think, say, and do. It can be argued that the opinions of other people aren't important, or the way they think of you doesn't matter, but having a good reputation is crucial in every aspect of your professional and personal life. You see, if a potential employer sees you as unreliable, or even dishonest, why would they employ you? If friends, or potential new friends, see you as hard work or no fun to be around, why would they choose to spend time with you?

This is why your name is your most valuable asset. It's more precious than all other assets put together, be it your home, your job, your business, your car, or anything else that money can buy. And this is why establishing a good name and reputation for yourself is so important if you are to stand out in life for all the right reasons. Your reputation is a tool that can be used to help you achieve your full potential in life. A good reputation can open doors for you; a bad reputation can lead to those doors remaining locked, or slamming in your face!

Establishing a Good Reputation

If you want to have a good reputation, you need to earn it. A good name is not something you can buy, and keeping a good name requires consistency in everything you do. It takes time to establish a reputation, but all it takes to destroy a good reputation is one ill-judged moment. What you *say* is of no value if it's not what you *do*. Saying you're a hard worker means nothing if you don't back up your words with actions. Saying you're a loyal friend means nothing if you fail to demonstrate it when it matters most in your friendships. It's what you do that becomes your reputation. If you often say one thing but then do another, all you establish is a reputation for being someone who can't be trusted or relied upon.

In fact, establishing a good reputation shouldn't be your goal at all. Your goal should be to live your life in a way that allows you to become the best version of yourself it's possible to be. If you always strive to be your best and do your best, your good reputation becomes a natural by-product. It's not about striving for perfection; it's simply striving to be the best you can be.

When you have a good name...

Your reputation speaks for you.

In today's world of public opinion effectively being judge and jury, your good reputation earns you support from others, even when you're not there to speak up for yourself. You can't stop malicious people having their say, but your reputation can lead to others rising to your defence.

You have a powerful source of motivation.

Having a good name to live up to provides motivation to always be and do your best. There may be times when you feel your good reputation is undeserved but knowing that it's there helps to keep you focused on your strengths rather than dwelling on weaknesses. Remember, establishing a good name isn't the end goal, it's a by-product of always trying to improve yourself.

You inspire others.

Striving to be your best in all you do makes you an inspirational role model. Demonstrating that it's not about perfection, it's about constantly learning and improving, makes you a positive role model.

It's worth reiterating that establishing a good reputation shouldn't be your end goal, and that caring about your reputation shouldn't lead to manipulating the way others see you. It's not about creating false impressions; it's about allowing your everyday actions to speak volumes about who you are and what you truly stand for in life. Human beings will always judge one another, so in establishing a good name for yourself, you are ensuring your true colours always shine through.

Establishing a good reputation is at the heart of Monty Roberts' successful career as a horse trainer. In his book,

The Man Who Listens to Horses, he tells his story of growing up as the son of a horse trainer in California, and riding before he could walk. It was the 1940s and Western films were at the peak of their popularity, giving him the opportunity to ride as a stunt double for child actors. Success in rodeos and horse shows followed, and Monty's reputation as an accomplished horseman was established.

However, it had always been his dream to become a horse trainer himself. He now had a wife and family to support, so it felt like the right time to get serious about going into the business. His experience as a rider was clear, but he was an inexperienced horse trainer and clients were few and far between. With only four horses to train, he wasn't bringing in enough money to survive. Unsure of his future, Monty was given an opportunity to work as an apprentice under one of the most well-known and respected trainers in the area, Don Dodge. At the end of the 10-week apprenticeship, Don met with Monty. Two of Monty's horses had been with him at Don's, and Don now told him that when he got home, he should tell the owner of one of them that he was wasting his money having Monty train his horse. This was because he believed the horse was never going to make the grade.

Monty was reluctant to take this advice because it would mean having only three clients. When he asked why he should lose a client in this way, Don told him that the most important thing he could do as a trainer was always tell owners the truth about their horses. He believed that being honest would soon bring in more than enough business to replace the loss.

Monty did as Don had suggested and called the client. The client didn't like what he was being told and yelled at length, saying, 'You useless son of a gun, you wouldn't know a good horse if it leapt up between your legs. That's the last horse you'll ever get from me!'

Several days later, Monty's phone rang. A voice on the other end said, 'Hello, Mr Gray here, Joe Gray.' He went on, 'I was having lunch with Mr Williams yesterday. He was complaining about you, but from what I heard you must be about the only honest trainer I ever heard of. Well, I know that horse of his wasn't any good, and I just want to take a flyer on you. I have this horse I want to send to you; it's called My Blue Heaven.'

This proved to be the turning point. Monty's client list grew along with his reputation – not only as an excellent trainer, but an honest one.

Making a Mark for Yourself

Making a good name for yourself is part and parcel of making a mark for yourself in life. To be able to live a fulfilled and contented life, you need to find your own path to being all you can be. Whatever it is you want to achieve in life, or in your career, there's no space for sitting back and resting on your laurels. To make a mark, you must always give your best, and if you always put a best effort into all you do, your best will keep on getting better. There's a famous quote attributed to St Jerome that makes this point beautifully: "Good. Better. Best. Never let it rest. 'Til your good is better and your better is best". You see, being your best self is not about being *the* best at everything, it's about being and doing *your* best in everything.

Just like establishing a good reputation, making a mark for yourself in life is standing out for the right reasons. For example, in a job interview, what will make you stand out from all the other candidates with the same list of qualifications on paper? In a workplace environment, what will make you stand out from your work colleagues when the opportunity to go for promotion arises? In both scenarios, the answer is your character. As Abraham Lincoln once said, "Character is like a tree and reputation like a shadow. The shadow is what we think of it; the tree is the real thing".

Good Character Traits

The positive character traits that make you stand out from the crowd include:

Honesty

Honesty is more than simply telling the truth. It's being truthful to who you are and living the truth in all you do. Genuine honesty makes you a straightforward and trustworthy person, so being honest is being authentic.

The Greek story of *The Woodcutter and the Axe* is a tale of honesty always being the best policy. One day, a woodcutter accidentally dropped his axe into a river. The axe was his only means of making a living, so he sat down on the riverbank in tears. The god, Hermes, saw him and took pity on him, diving into the river to retrieve the lost axe. He surfaced clutching an axe made of solid gold and asked, 'Is this the axe you lost?' The woodcutter shook his head and said no, and then shook his head again when Hermes brought out an axe of silver. Only when his old axe was retrieved did the woodcutter claim it. Hermes was so impressed by the woodcutter's honesty that he gifted all three axes to him.

When an envious neighbour heard of this good fortune, he threw his own axe into the river and sat wailing on the riverbank awaiting its return. Once again, Hermes brought a golden axe to the surface, asking if this was what had been lost. The greedy neighbour eagerly claimed it as his, but his dishonesty meant he was denied it – and also the return of his own.

Authenticity

Being authentic is being "the real thing". There's no posturing or pretence, and you are sincere in everything you do. Authenticity requires self-awareness and being your real self means being able to show vulnerability at times – no one is perfect.

Authentic leadership is an increasingly popular concept in the workplace. Its origins stem all the way back to Ancient Greece, with philosophers of the time believing authenticity to be an important state of being as it represented taking control of your own destiny and being true to who you really are. Stemming from the Greek word *authentikos*, authentic means genuine, and in today's world, being an authentic leader requires three cornerstone qualities:

- Always being true to yourself and your values.
- Being open and honest with other people.
- Choosing to do the right thing, professionally and morally, not just the thing that stands to benefit you most as the leader.

Authenticity was closely linked to the Ancient Greek cardinal values. Those values were:

Prudence – considering all possible courses of action before acting in a fair-minded manner.

Temperance – staying in control of emotions at all times.

Justice – dealing with other people in a fair manner.

Fortitude – having the inner courage to always do the right thing.

To the Ancient Greeks, authentic leadership was not only morally right, but it was also a means of improving themselves as leaders and improving their relationships with others.

A good example of authentic leadership in action can be found in the story of Steve Jobs and Apple. He was always true and honest with himself, and he always did what he believed to be the right thing, not just for Apple but for the common good. In his 2012 biography of Steve Jobs, author Walter Isaacson describes him as "famously impatient, petulant, and tough with the people around him" and then writes: "But these traits and behaviours stemmed from a passion for perfection, and even though he was tough on people, they stayed with Apple because they believed in his vision. Even with his personality flaws, Jobs was surrounded by loyal colleagues who had been inspired by him for years, and a loving family. Jobs believed that Apple products should be great. Jobs stated that his passion was to build an enduring company where people were motivated to make great products. He was never afraid to tell his staff that their ideas were wrong or dumb and he would refocus them on the true vision for Apple".

In one quote included in the biography, Steve Jobs said, "I don't think I run roughshod over people, but if something sucks, I tell people to their face. It's my job to be honest". The author writes, "His strive for perfection of his innovations led to loss of short-term profits because he refused to use another company's 'uninspired' hardware run with apple software, over fears that unapproved apps and content might 'pollute the perfection of an Apple device'". Jobs' focus on product over profits is what inspired his colleagues and led to products that revolutionised the tech industry, and also many other industries. These are the ways that Steve Jobs demonstrated authenticity as a leader. It is through his authenticity that Jobs inspired his colleagues.

Integrity

With integrity, you stay true to yourself and what you stand for in all you do – even when there is no one else around to see you doing it. You are guided by strong moral principles and core values, and you live your life by them.

The story of tennis champion Andy Roddick provides a powerful example of integrity in action. In 2005, he was playing against Fernando Verdasco of Spain in the Italia Masters tennis tournament. As the number one seed, Roddick was favourite to win, and he didn't disappoint his fans. He dominated the match, but then, just when he had triple match point, he found himself struggling to return his opponent's second serve. However, the linesman called Verdasco's serve out, meaning Roddick was awarded the game, set, and match.

The crowd cheered and Verdasco ran to the net to congratulate Roddick on his victory, but then something unexpected happened. Roddick knew the ball had not been out. He knew it had hit the line. The ball had been in, despite the linesman, the crowd, the umpire, and his opponent believing it to be out. He could have kept quiet and simply accepted the victory being awarded to him. In the rules of tennis, honour calls are not expected, but Roddick chose to approach the umpire and inform him of the error. He pointed out the mark on the clay that backed up his statement, and the umpire then reversed his call to award the point to Verdasco.

Against all odds, Verdasco came back strong to win the match. Many sportswriters have since commented that Roddick's integrity as a player cost him tens of thousands of dollars that day, and potentially many tens of thousands more as he may have gone on to win the tournament. However, integrity was clearly valued more than money, and honesty more than a win. As one of the top players in the world at the time, Roddick's loss was undoubtedly unexpected, but while he may have lost a match that day, he gained a phenomenal reputation across the sport of tennis – and beyond.

Responsibility

Responsibility and accountability go hand in hand. You always follow through on commitments or obligations, even when they're challenging. You accept responsibility for your own actions because you know that your thoughts, emotions, and consequent behaviours are always your choice. All of the above character traits along with responsibility make you someone who can always be relied upon to do what they say they will do.

Motivational speaker and author Stephen Covey puts it this way: "Look at the word responsibility – response-ability – the ability to choose your response. Highly proactive people recognise that responsibility. They do not blame circumstances, conditions, or conditioning for their behaviour. Their behaviour is a product of their own conscious choice, based on values, rather than a product of their conditions, based on feeling".

Respectfulness

With respectfulness you treat others as you would wish to be treated yourself. You accept differences and treat everyone with the same degree of courtesy, kindness, dignity, and due deference. You also respect your own worth and accept that everyone has flaws.

African Wisdom is the title of a book written by Ellen K Kuzwayo. In its pages, she tells stories of her childhood and the wisdom passed down to her through her mother's actions.

Of the many interactions I had with my mother those many years ago, one stands out with clarity. I remember the occasion when mother sent me to the main road, about twenty yards away from the homestead, to invite a passing group of seasonal work-seekers home for a meal. She instructed me to take a container along and collect dry cow dung for making a fire. I was then to prepare the meal for the group of work-seekers.

The thought of making an open fire outside at midday, cooking in a large three-legged pot in that intense heat, was sufficient to upset even an angel. I did not manage to conceal my feelings from my mother and, after serving the group, she called me to the veranda where she usually sat to attend to her sewing and knitting.

Looking straight into my eyes, she said, 'Tsholofelo, why did you sulk when I requested you to prepare a meal for those poor destitute people?' Despite my attempt to deny her allegation, and using the heat of the fire and the sun as an excuse for my alleged behaviour, Mother, giving me a firm look, said, 'Lonao ga lo na nko' – 'A foot has no nose.' It means you cannot detect what trouble may lie ahead of you.

Had I denied this group of people a meal, it may have happened that, in my travels sometime in the future, I found myself at the mercy of those very individuals.

As if that was not enough to shame me, mother continued, 'Motho ke motho ka motho yo mongwe.' The literal meaning: a person is a person because of another person.

Humility

In short, humility is not considering yourself to be better than anyone else or "too good" for certain situations in life. Self-confidence is a positive character trait when coupled with humility, allowing you to strive for more while appreciating all you have, rather than simply *expecting* more to be handed to you on a plate.

Mahatma Gandhi's story perhaps epitomises humility. He devoted his life to serving the poorest of the poor. He carried soil on his head, cleaned his own ashram by hand, and spun cotton cloth to make clothing for himself. He once said, "One must become as humble as the dust before he can discover truth".

Perseverance

Call it perseverance, persistence, or determination, this character trait keeps you steadfastly on track to becoming all you can be in life, and fulfilling whatever you discover your purpose to be… taking us full circle to making a mark for yourself.

At the age of 65, Colonel Sanders was living off social security checks and had little to his name besides a beat-up old car. Determined to change his life, he thought about what he had to offer that may be of benefit to other people. What he had was a fried chicken recipe that he knew family and friends loved. Leaving his home in Kentucky, he set off to pitch his recipe to restaurant owners across America. After visiting 1009 locations, not one had taken him up on his offer. That's 1009 rejections, but he persevered. He believed in himself and his recipe, and he kept going. On his 1010th pitch, he got a *yes*. The rest, as they say, is history.

The Positive Impact of Good Character

Adding to the list above, fairness, generosity, and compassion are positive character traits that can have a positive impact on society at every level. We can all demonstrate these traits in all walks of life, with the smallest of acts often making the biggest of differences in the lives of others.

Keanu Reeves is a man made famous by his acting roles in numerous films, not least the *Matrix* franchise. His successful career may have made him wealthy, but his good character has made him a man admired and respected far beyond his industry. To give just one example, instead of accumulating even greater wealth through his profit-share deals in the *Matrix* sequels, he chose to share those profits among the workers in the special effects and costume design departments, stating that he believed they had been the ones who really made the film.

British actor Benedict Cumberbatch is another positive example of good character in the film and television industry. As his fame and starring roles became bigger, he could have been laughing all the way to the bank, but his moral compass saw him take a different stance. He chose to advocate for women and equal pay in the film industry, saying, "If she's not paid the same as the men, I'm not doing it".

James Doty is a name that's perhaps not quite so well known. He is an American neurosurgeon, university professor, entrepreneur, and founder of the Center for Compassion and Altruism Research and Education. Success in his early career gave him a net worth of around $75 million, and being a generous man, he pledged $30 million to charitable causes. However, the dot-com crash of 2000-2001 hit his investments hard, and he lost almost everything – but he still had the pledged stock.

His circumstances had changed beyond recognition and lawyers advised him that people would understand if he needed to go back on his pledge. No one would expect him to follow through, he could change his mind. After considering his options, James chose to stick by his pledge and give away all that was left of his fortune. In later years, he would say, "One of the persistent myths in our society is that money will make you happy. Growing up poor, I thought that money would give me everything I did not have: control, power, love. When I finally had all the money I had ever dreamed of, I discovered that it did not make me happy... At that moment I realised that the only way that money can bring happiness is to give it away".

Pledging to give away $30 million became a pledge to give away all that he had. It may not have been his initial intention, but he stuck by his commitment to give. The irony of it all is that only after giving money did he find the happiness he thought he would find in having money.

These examples show that individuals with good character always stick by what they believe in, and stand up for what they believe to be right. For some, success in life may be linked to wealth and fame, but for all of us, being the best version of ourselves we can be in all we do is all it takes to make a mark for ourselves and stand out for the right reasons.

Being Your Best

You already know that being your best self is not about being *the* best at everything, it's about being and doing *your* best in everything. Good character makes you stand out, and you can work on developing stand-out character traits by focusing on a few key areas:

Be Positive: Being enthusiastic, confident, and upbeat will always make you stand out for the right reasons. Be someone who looks for the positives in every situation, and you become someone other people like to be around. No one wants to spend time with someone who only ever complains or looks for problems.

Be Engaging: Being friendly and genuinely interested in other people makes you approachable and therefore someone who can build relationships easily. Being someone who can connect with others will always help you to create good first impressions and stand out from the crowd in a positive way.

Be a Good Communicator: Being able to express yourself positively is the perfect way to let your true colours shine through. However, it's important to remember that good communication goes beyond simply talking, it also includes listening. Being a good listener goes a long way towards making yourself memorable for all the right reasons, and all it takes is a little respect. Be fully engaged with the person you're listening to by maintaining appropriate eye contact, and always let them know they have your full attention.

In summary, **standing out for the right reasons** is showing yourself in your best light and always striving to be and do your best. In so doing, you begin to establish a good name for yourself, you build a good reputation, and you continue to demonstrate the good character traits that make you who you are. As you continue to read through the following chapters, you will learn that developing these standout traits gives you all you need to:

- Attract the trust and respect of others.
- Positively influence others.
- Change your perspective on failure.
- Sustain your motivation through tough times.
- Elevate your confidence, self-respect, and self-esteem.
- Stay committed to values and goals in life.
- Create foundations for happy, healthy relationships.
- And improve your chances of success in all areas of life.

Chapter 1 Standout Points

❶ Standing out for the right reasons is all about who you are and how you present yourself in what you do.

❷ Establishing a good name for yourself is a key element of standing out for the right reasons; your name is the reputation that goes before you.

❸ If you want to have a good reputation, you need to earn it. It's not about striving for perfection; it's simply striving to be the best you can be.

❹ To be able to live a fulfilled and contented life, you need to find your own path to being all you can be.

❺ Good character makes you stand out, and you can work on developing stand-out character traits by being positive, being engaging, and being a good communicator.

Chapter 2

The Importance of Morals and Values

Morals are the guidelines we live by. They help us to develop a strong sense of right and wrong, and to make good choices in life. They do this by teaching us how to behave in a socially acceptable way, how to treat other people around us, and to understand the consequences of our actions. Morals are therefore something we acquire through experience and from the example shown to us by the people who care for us when we're growing up. We then gain further experience from the wider community as we get older and interact with different people, and this is why the morals held by one individual can be quite different to those held by another.

Universal Morals

Morals aren't necessarily fixed; they can shift and change. An individual's morals may be influenced by cultural or religious beliefs, and those beliefs can vary hugely around the globe. Times also change, and morals with them. What may once have been deemed immoral may become acceptable in a modern society, and vice versa. However, research carried out by anthropologists at the University of Oxford has revealed seven morals that can be considered universal. They are:

- Love and help your family
- Defer to superiors and authority

- Help your group/community
- Be fair and divide resources fairly
- Return favours
- Respect the property of others
- Be brave

There are many other examples of moral behaviour that most people will have been encouraged to abide by. These include telling the truth, being polite, not stealing, having empathy for others, and treating other people as you'd like to be treated yourself. In short, morals encompass the sorts of behaviours and attitudes we're brought up to believe in as being the "right" way to live your life.

Morals, Values, and Principles

The morals you live by govern the way you behave and the choices you make in life. For this reason, the terms morals, values, and principles are often used interchangeably. The things you value and the principles you stand by in life help to influence your every decision, motivating you to do the right thing, but there are subtle differences between the terms. If we think of morals as right or proper behaviour, then values are what we believe to be right or wrong behaviour. In other words, we learn morals through society or religion, but values come from within.

The Moral of the Story...

Most of us grow up hearing or reading stories that teach us about rights and wrongs in life. Aesop's fables are famous examples of stories with morals. *The Boy that*

Cried Wolf teaches the dangers of telling lies; *The Tortoise and the Hare* teaches that slow and steady can win the race, or that perseverance can win over arrogance; and *The Goose that Laid the Golden Eggs* teaches the perils of greed.

However, there are also plenty of moral dilemmas presented in story form, each serving to demonstrate that what you deem to be right or wrong behaviour is ultimately decided by your values. The tale of Robin Hood is a great example. Is stealing from the rich to give to the poor morally right or wrong? If you put the story into a more modern context and imagine you've witnessed a robbery, it's perhaps easier to consider your answer. A bank has been robbed, but the thief has donated all of the stolen money to an orphanage. You know who committed the crime. What do you do? If you report what you know to the police, there's every chance the money will be taken from the orphanage and returned to the bank. Without funds, children remain in need. However, reporting to the police is arguably the right thing to do. What would *you* do?

In the storybooks, Robin Hood is considered a hero. Stealing is morally bad behaviour, but giving to people in need is morally good, so the general message in the prose is that his end justifies the means – but can the same thinking ever be applied to real life?

Real World Moral Dilemmas

In everyday life, it's often the small dilemmas we face and the on-the-spot decisions we make that shine a light on our true moral character. Here are a few examples to consider, but try not to ponder over each one for too long. Go with your gut response!

You've just bought something at your local corner shop with cash. You've been given too much change. Do you keep quiet, or do you point out the error?

A package is delivered to your home that should have gone to a different address. The label on it indicates it's an item you want for yourself, but can't afford to buy. Do you keep it, or do you notify the delivery company/ take it to the intended address?

A neighbour on your street leaves their dog outside in all kinds of weather. You notice it often looks miserable, and the water bowl appears to be empty. Do you report what you believe may be happening, or do you keep quiet?

One of your friends is about to drive home after a party. You know they have been drinking alcohol all evening, but they refuse to hand over their car keys. What do you do?

Your lunch keeps going missing from your workplace kitchen. You think you know who is taking it. Do you confront them, report them to management, or say nothing?

You buy several items of clothing at a branch of Next (or another big retail brand). When you get home, you notice that one of the items is not on the till receipt.

Do you return to the store to pay for it, or do you let it go?

Your friend is in a new relationship and ecstatically happy. However, you know her new boyfriend has a bad reputation for breaking hearts. Do you tell her, risking your friendship, or do you say nothing, risking your friend getting hurt?

You see, there isn't always a clear right or wrong response in every situation, it comes down to your character and your values. Sometimes you need to consider your response to bigger and more complex dilemmas to get to the heart of what you truly value. Here's a popular example:

Imagine you are on a cruise. You get caught in a violent storm that causes catastrophic damage and all passengers are informed they must prepare to abandon ship. Everyone is instructed to make their way to the lifeboats. As you approach the boats, you notice that some queues are shorter than others and some passengers are getting on board faster than others. You know that you are a strong and capable person so do you join a queue with elderly passengers needing help that you could give; a queue with families and young children that you could perhaps assist; or do you join the shortest queue of other capable people, perhaps giving yourself the greatest chance of survival?

This sort of dilemma is, by design, a little more difficult to imagine than some of the earlier everyday scenarios. It may take greater consideration, but taking a moment to put yourself into a difficult situation – albeit in your mind – can go a long way towards identifying what matters most to you, and what actions are likely to follow your thought processes. There are no right and wrong answers, only answers guided by your personal character and values.

Strong Moral Character

"Character is that which reveals moral purpose, exposing the class of things a man chooses and avoids" – Aristotle.

Your character can be defined as the qualities or behaviours that identify you as an individual, but as the above quote suggests, *your* character is only ever as strong as *your* core values and beliefs. The way you think and behave is always your choice, so this means your character is your choice. Becoming someone of strong moral character isn't something that happens by accident, it's something you need to intentionally do.

When you choose to be someone of strong moral character, you choose to:

Build a solid reputation: In both your personal and professional life, your reputation goes before you. As you already know, your reputation is a tool that can be used to help you achieve your full potential in life. Establishing a good reputation is part and parcel of attracting the people and opportunities into your life that will help you to be all you can be.

Be trustworthy and reliable: A strong character is a reliable character. When you choose to develop good moral character, you become someone others can trust and rely on. You are open, honest, and you can always be counted on to be true to your word.

Be a positive role model: Strong moral character puts you in a position to positively influence the thoughts and actions of others. You earn respect by showing respect. You always do right by others, and you stand firmly by what you believe in.

Live a purposeful life: Having strong moral character means living a life you can be proud of. You are driven to be the best you can be and to do your best in all you do, but never at the expense of others. It's all about who you are, not what you have.

In short, strong moral character adds up to a life of happiness and success. Traits such as honesty, integrity, and loyalty earn respect and allow trusting relationships to form. Being trustworthy and reliable helps create a good reputation, and having a good name opens up doors to a world of opportunities.

The Story of Honest Abe

Abraham Lincoln is a name synonymous with strong moral character. He grew up in a remote rural environment where his father farmed. In those days, young boys tended to do as their fathers had done – and their fathers before them – but Abe knew farming was not for him. He was a thoughtful and independent boy, and even though there was no formal schooling available to him, he chose to educate himself through reading. He read books that taught him about great thinkers and doers. He read not only for pleasure but also as a form of discipline, reading the same few books over and over again so that he would fully absorb the lessons contained within the pages. He read to understand grammar, geometry, and to learn about what others thought, said, and did, and, perhaps, most importantly, he read to find out *why* and *how* they did it.

He was conscious of the limitations of his rural upbringing, but Abe was determined to become the best he could be and to realise his full potential in life. He read about individuals who had succeeded despite struggles and setbacks, and he learned all he could about thinking, speaking, and acting for himself. He made a conscious decision to be and do better, and intentionally set out to become his best.

In his early working days, Abe worked as a clerk in a general store. It was there that he earned himself the nickname of "Honest Abe" as it's reported he would walk for miles at the end of his day to correct any miscalculations that had led to a customer being short-changed – even if only by a penny. He always delivered the correct change to the customer personally.

His honesty and integrity became his reputation, even when he later became a lawyer. Many considered law to be a disreputable profession, but Abe's good name went before him. Colleagues had absolute faith and confidence in him to tell the truth, and in some notes he wrote for a lecture given to students of law, he wrote, "Dismiss the popular belief that lawyers are necessarily dishonest... Resolve to be honest at all events; and if, in your own judgment, you cannot be an honest lawyer, resolve to be honest without being a lawyer. Choose some other occupation".

By the time Abraham Lincoln was elected 16th president of the United States in 1860, he had established himself as one of Illinois' most successful and distinguished lawyers. Everyone, even his enemies, knew where they stood with Honest Abe, and his sincerity in all he said and did was beyond question.

"Whatever you are, be a good one" – Abraham Lincoln.

What we can all learn from Abraham Lincoln's story is that an individual's circumstances don't dictate their character. He was born into a poor farming family, but *chose* to be more. In every job he had, he chose to be his best and do his best. He chose to live his life by a moral code built around his values and beliefs, and he stood by those beliefs in everything he said and did.

Choose Integrity

It's not always easy to stand by what you believe in, especially in a world where social media "influencers" constantly attempt to convince you that you *need* to believe something else. It can feel virtually impossible to remain true to your real self when external pressures seem to pull you in every direction – just to fit in with others – but having integrity allows you to stand firm.

It's often said that integrity is doing the right thing, even when no one is watching. It's a quality that demonstrates your belief in yourself and your strong moral principles. You have a firm sense of what's right and what's wrong, and you're not about to be "influenced" into thinking, saying, or doing anything you don't believe to be the right thing.

When you have integrity:

You are reliable: People will take you at your word in both your personal and professional life.

Your good reputation goes before you: Your reliability and trustworthiness become synonymous with who you are.

You do your best: You are always striving to be and do your best, irrespective of the opinions or beliefs of others.

You grow in confidence: You feel secure in who you are and what you stand for.

You are authentic: You always stick by what you value, and you never pretend to be someone or something you're not.

You establish good relationships: Authenticity and integrity will always attract others to you.

You gain respect: Your good reputation is maintained in all you say and do, earning you the personal and professional respect of others, as well as self-respect from knowing your decisions and actions are guided by what you truly believe and value.

You inspire and lead others: Your honesty and ability to take responsibility for your thoughts and actions will inspire and motivate others to follow your example and do their best.

You sleep well: Being true to yourself in all you do allows you to end each day with a clear conscience. Dishonesty will only ever lead to sleepless nights!

And you feel at peace: Not compromising who you are or what you believe in just to fit in with others brings a sense of inner calm. Choosing to always be honest with yourself and others avoids the turmoil of pretending to be someone you're not.

Integrity is not a trait that can be switched on and off depending on where you are or what you're doing. Remember, it's doing the right thing, even when no one is watching.

Here's an example of integrity in the workplace:

> Lily is a digital marketer, and part of a team working on a very large project that needs to be completed by Thursday. Things go well at the start of the week with the whole team working hard to meet the deadline, but there's a noticeable

dip in enthusiasm and productivity by Wednesday. Lily realises that her workmates are slowing down, and then when their marketing manager informs them that he needs to be away from the office for the rest of Wednesday afternoon, she can't help but notice them breathing a sigh of relief and effectively grinding to a halt. It now seems that Lily is the only one left working on the project – what should she do? Well, she could have adopted an if-you-can't-beat-them-join-them attitude, but her integrity saw her take a different approach. Doing the right thing meant doing her best, but she knew she couldn't do all the work on her own. She did her best to politely encourage the others to get the project back on track, and even though only a few of the team chose to join her, their efforts allowed them to get the job done.

Lily met with her manager on Thursday morning to hand over the completed project, giving her the opportunity to explain what had happened. In response to these happenings, the manager put accountability checkpoints in place for the whole team, and promoted Lily to team supervisor. Her integrity not only made it possible to meet the project deadline, but it also led to improvements in her workplace.

Morals and Values make the World a Better Place

The discussion over what's morally right or wrong is possibly one that will never fully conclude, but the importance of morals and values is universally understood. Having a sense of morality is choosing to do the right thing for the right reasons; it's choosing to treat other people fairly and with kindness, or to simply treat others as you'd wish to be treated yourself. If we could all do this – all the time – wouldn't it make the world a better place?

Okay, it's perhaps unrealistic to imagine a world where everyone shares the same values and *always* chooses to do the right thing. But – and it's an important but – while you can't control what other people choose to do, you *can* choose to take control over what you do.

Knowing what's right and wrong can help you to make better decisions in life. After all, you need to know what you believe to be right and wrong to be able to make decisions that are consistent with your values. Without strong morals and values, simple choices and decisions become more difficult to make. As someone poetic once put it, "Without morality, we are adrift in a sea of meaningless decisions". Your morality guides the choices you make – what should you do, how should you behave, how should you respond to a situation? Without morality, the choices and decisions you make can only be guided by whatever you believe serves *you* best. This would lead to a very lonely life in which you'd struggle to form any true or meaningful relationships with other people.

Better or Best?

It's one thing to *say* that you value honesty and integrity, but are you always true to your word in all you *do*?

Do you always *do* your best, or do you sometimes only do what you need to do to be better than the others around you? Think about it – is being the best of a bad bunch really being your best? Is being the "winner" really being your best if you've given less than your best at every stage along the way, and you just happened to be better than anyone else on the day? If you've compromised what you value, you haven't done your best.

Keep Striving

There's an old story about a young boy making a determined effort to be his best...

One day, a young boy walked into a corner shop where there was a payphone. He was too small to reach it, so he found himself a box to stand on. The shop owner watched him with a curious smile. The boy dialled a number, and he was then heard asking whoever had answered if they would hire him to cut their grass. The shop owner assumed the answer must have been no because the boy then said, 'I will cut your lawn better than whoever is cutting it now. I can also sweep your path, your patio, and your driveway. Your lawn will be the prettiest in the neighbourhood!'

His pitch was so good, the shop owner couldn't help but listen. When the boy hung up the phone, he asked him, 'Well, did you get the job?'

'No, I didn't,' he replied. 'They said they're happy with the service they're getting right now.'

This made the shop owner feel sad for the boy. Surely his persistent attitude deserved to be rewarded in some way. 'I can give you a job,' he said.

To the shop owner's surprise, the boy politely declined the offer with a smile. 'No thank you,' he said, 'I am the one cutting their grass already. I was just calling to check they're happy with my work.'

The moral in this tale is that to be your best, you need to be honest with yourself. This means evaluating your strengths and your weaknesses, and comparing yourself with no one other than yourself – as the person you want to be. Remember the wise words of Honest Abe: "Whatever you are, be a good one".

It's true that an individual's morality may be guided by cultural traditions, but each one of us is ultimately responsible for our own moral standards and values. Morals may vary from person to person, mainly through the influences of upbringing and cultural norms, but everyone has some sense of morality. Being true to yourself and what you believe to be morally right is the only route to making *your* world a better place.

Strong morals and values help you to stand out from the crowd.

Chapter 2 Standout Points

❶ Morals are the guidelines we live by. They help us to develop a strong sense of right and wrong, and to make good choices in life.

❷ An individual's morals may be influenced by cultural or religious beliefs, and those beliefs can vary hugely around the globe.

❸ There isn't always a clear "right" or "wrong" response in every situation, it comes down to *your* character and *your* values.

❹ Your character is only ever as strong as your core values and beliefs.

❺ Having a sense of morality is choosing to do the right thing for the right reasons; it's choosing to treat other people fairly and with kindness, or to simply treat others as you'd wish to be treated yourself.

Chapter 3

The Decline of Moral Values and Its Impact on Society

Numerous studies suggest that many people believe moral values to be in decline. They believe this because they see a change in the way people behave and interact with one another, and a general shift in attitude away from helping one another to looking out only for themselves. For some, basic kindness appears to be in decline, and the question they ask is, "Do we no longer care about other people?"

What Happened to Human Kindness?

Anyone might be forgiven for seeing today's world as a place where looking out for number one has become the norm, and trampling over other people to get ahead is simply part of the process. The world is constantly changing, but does getting ahead in life *really* need to be at the expense of kindness towards others?

To answer the question of what happened to human kindness, there are quite a few changes to consider. These are...

The pace of life: It's fair to say that we're living an increasingly fast-paced life. We rush from place to place and fill our days with meetings and appointments, but could it be that we're now always in such a hurry that we've stopped taking the time to pay attention to other people or to simply listen to others?

Advances in technology: We use technology to communicate *without* having to meet or talk to someone face-to-face. Emails, texts, and social media posts have taken over from phone calls or in-person meetings, thereby diluting the human connection. Today's technology also provides a means of avoiding interactions with other people on a daily basis, or getting involved in other people's daily dramas – and passing comment anonymously. Could it be that the lack of face-to-face connection has created a lack of consideration for the impact of our words on others?

Apps and emojis: Following on from the above, in the days before there was an app for everything, we had far more need – or opportunity – to interact with other people on a daily basis. Today, we can order food, book tickets, make appointments, buy groceries, clothes, furniture – and even look for love – without having to talk to anyone in person. The common courtesies of everyday face-to-face interactions are becoming a thing of the past as automated services don't need a please and thank you, and they don't need an exchange of smiles or pleasantries about the weather! Emojis can even make the process of sending a text message even faster. Why bother taking the time to speak to someone on the phone or type a meaningful message when you can simply select an appropriate emoji and call it done?

A "me-first" attitude: "Doing well for yourself" appears to have become more important than *how* you do it. Getting to the top of the career ladder at all or any cost appears to be an attitude that young people are encouraged to adopt. Workplaces have become competition fields with everyone claiming to be a "team player", yet always looking out for themselves. Winning is the goal, but the competitiveness of the "me-first" attitude or selfishness of the "what's in it for me?" attitude has perhaps spilled over into all areas of life, leading to a lack of consideration or concern for other people.

Rising crime?: It can be argued that crime rates are on the increase, but it can also be argued that it's the reporting of crimes that has increased, rather than the number of crimes being committed. However, it's fair to say that fear of crime, and general suspicion around strangers, has created a greater tendency to keep ourselves to ourselves, especially in big cities. Where once it may have been the norm to stop and offer help to someone looking like they might need it, *not* getting involved and perhaps even looking the other way is now a much more likely response.

Cultural norms: Adding to the above, there's a general shift away from interaction with other people to avoiding them whenever possible. Grandparents in today's world may remember times when neighbours popped in on one another, conversations were held over garden fences, and back doors could safely be left unlocked. Now, neighbours often never see one another, let alone strike up conversations, and doors are never left unlocked – even when people are at home! Cultural norms have changed. Respect for elders and those in authority has changed. News stories of police officers, nurses, and teachers having to deal with abusive behaviour are common, and in many areas, where once there was neighbourliness, politeness, and general kindness towards others in the local community, there is now hostility, rudeness, and no community spirit whatsoever. In short, no one wants to risk being the "nice guy" who ends up being taken advantage of. Being kind makes you an easy target – and being aggressive, pushy, and often downright rude have somehow become "admirable" qualities that all go-getters need to get ahead in life.

Once again, does getting ahead in life *really* need to be at the expense of kindness towards others? The answer is no, but it's clear that moral values such as kindness are no longer as universal as they perhaps once were. The finger of blame can be pointed at technology and social media to an extent, but the behaviours of world leaders and other influential people must also be questioned. Anonymous posting on the internet means people can say anything, generally without consequence, and the lack of ability to filter then creeps into offline life. Political figures tearing strips off one another in public and so-called celebrities sharing their (often controversial or misinformed) opinions with the world only adds to the mistaken belief that being rude, greedy, selfish, intolerant, disrespectful, angry, and a liar is acceptable behaviour if you want to be someone in life.

Who Do You Want to Be?

What's more important to you – being *the* best, or being *your* best? In the game of life, is it more important to win, or to play well? Sportswriter Grantland Rice once said, "It's not whether you win or lose, it's how you play the game". These are wise words, and they are an important reminder that standing out in life should be standing out for the right reasons.

Actor Brian Blessed is well known around the world. He's not only famous for his acting roles and larger-than-life personality, but also for his many adventures, including attempts to climb Mount Everest. Three times he tried, never quite reaching the summit. Each attempt was made without supplemental oxygen, and he was already in his late 50s on his first attempt. This makes him a remarkable individual, but the most remarkable aspect of his story is that he turned back on one ascent to save the life of a fellow climber. Doing the right thing was more important than achieving a lifelong goal.

There are other stories of athletes giving up their own races to help a fellow athlete. After colliding in a 5000-metre track race, two athletes found themselves on the ground. Abbey D'Agostino of the USA and Nikki Hamblin of New Zealand collided after Nikki had to slow her pace suddenly to avoid contact with another runner. Abbey then ran into her from behind, and they both fell. Abbey was unhurt and could have attempted to make up lost ground, but she noticed that Nikki was hurt and needed help to get up. After the race, Nikki said, "When I went down it was like, 'what's happening? Why am I on the ground?' And suddenly there's this hand on my shoulder, like 'get up, get up, we have to finish this!' I'm so grateful to Abbey for doing that for me. That girl is the Olympic spirit right there." They came in last and second last in the race, but their good sportsmanship allowed both athletes to finish and make it through to the finals.

In one 10K Thailand Championship, a selfless runner sacrificed his own goal to help a fellow competitor. Just metres from the finish line, a runner found himself unable to take another step. Exhaustion took him to his knees. So close to the finish, a steady stream of competitors continued to run past him as they sprinted for the line, but one runner stopped short of the line and turned back to offer assistance. In helping another runner to his feet, he sacrificed his own finish time. Doing the right thing was more important than achieving a personal best race time.

The story of Ian Rosenberger is another good example of choosing to play well. In 2005, he was a contestant in the TV show *Survivor*. He and his fellow contestants were competing to win the prize pot of one million dollars. Out of the 20 that had started, Ian was now in the remaining three, and competing to be one of the last two survivors. He was clinging to an ocean buoy off the coast of Palau in a physically and mentally challenging test of endurance. All he had to do was hold on longer than the other two and he'd get through to the final. One of the three let go after five hours, leaving Ian and Tom, a contestant who had become Ian's best friend on the show. After 12 hours of holding on, Ian found the psychological challenge becoming even tougher than the physical challenge. He started thinking about how he had played the game, and about how much the million dollars meant to him. He knew that if he could win this challenge, he could win the prize pot. If he won this challenge, he won the right to choose which of the other two contestants to eliminate. If he eliminated Tom, the bigger threat as he saw it, he more or less created a clear path to victory for himself.

Alone with his thoughts, Ian's mind turned to the Scout Law. As an Eagle Scout, he knew that a Scout is always trustworthy and loyal... and it began to play on his mind that he had not demonstrated these qualities while playing the game. In an interview he gave after the show, he said, "I'd been backstabbing people and I was planning on doing that to my best friend in the game and realised I would lose that friend if I continued playing the game in the same way. Every time I pulled money out of the ATM account with the million dollars, it would bother me." He also said he began to think about the example he would be setting for his younger sister. "I thought about Scouting, and I thought about the people who would watch me win. They wouldn't have been proud." It was for these reasons that Ian let go of the buoy, quitting the challenge and the game as he asked Tom to eliminate him. Ian has since said, "I realised it's not just winning the million. It's *how* you win it. That is what I learned in Scouts. It's not just accomplishing something; how you accomplish it becomes important. I decided to bow out. That was because of the Scout Law – and because of my sister."

Ian realised that living his life according to the values he learned as a Scout was worth more to him than a million dollars. He has no regrets, but he has said, "I can't say that the cash wouldn't come in handy right now, but I'm completely happy with the decision I made. I don't regret it at all. It's only a million bucks. I left with pride and a story I could be proud of... although if I stayed, I wouldn't be eating ramen noodles every day as I am now!"

Choose to be a Positive Influence

The values you live your life by are *your* choice. Showing kindness to others is your choice; treating yourself and others with respect is your choice; caring for other people, and protecting the vulnerable is your choice, and so is *not* doing any of these things.

Think of it this way: paying attention to your carbon footprint is a hot topic in today's world. The more you can do to reduce it, the more you're doing to help save the planet. How about doing all you can to improve your emotional footprint? This means doing all you can to improve the way you treat other people and to reduce the potential for your words and actions to have a negative impact on them. Standing by good moral values creates a positive emotional footprint that can only serve to improve the quality of your life and the lives of everyone around you.

Remember, becoming someone of strong moral character isn't something that happens by accident, it's something you need to intentionally do. Are you intentionally kind to other people? Do your core values always guide you towards doing the right thing, or are your values subject to change depending on what you stand to gain or lose under the circumstances? Would you give up your seat on a crowded train to let a pregnant woman sit down? What about a young mum with a fractious toddler? Would you go to the aid of a child who appeared to be lost in a busy shopping centre? Would you knock on your neighbour's door and ask them if they wanted a lift with you to the supermarket? You see, there may be times when your thoughts and behaviours are guided by what's convenient, not necessarily what's kind!

Morality is Infectious

It can be argued that society today is, on the whole, less kind than in previous generations. It can be argued that the increasing busyness of modern life is to blame, and it can be argued that the way we respond to other people, especially strangers, has changed because we fear getting involved in someone else's business or we fear causing offense.

However, good morals are infectious. If you smile at someone, they'll often smile back at you in return. If you treat someone with kindness, they will often return that kindness, or extend it to someone else. You might say that "doing the right thing" can create a ripple effect – like dropping a pebble into still water – and the "right thing" becomes the norm for everyone touched by the expanding ripple. For example, parents can instil good morals into their children's lives; community leaders can lift the morality of their communities; and business leaders can create a healthy workplace culture that fosters positivity and best performances at every level. Strong values at the top of any organisation help to establish a foundation for its long-term success – and the personal and professional success of everyone involved.

The story of Mark Severino, a real estate investor in America, helps to demonstrate the real-life infectiousness of strong morals. In a business magazine article, he wrote: "I learned about morality from my father. When he was young, he was afflicted with polio and grew up physically handicapped. I never got to play ball, wrestle, or run around the park with him. He couldn't teach me how to ride a bicycle or shoot a basket. He lived a life where he couldn't do these things himself. From that, I learned the world is an unfair place. Morals are crucial because they are the code we live by, and how we see them ultimately influences our world. Without morality, I could be *bitter* and *angry,* having missed out on the idyllic childhood seen in every sitcom. But, because I care about morality and I was taught how to reframe life lessons, I believe that the world is unfair, and we must therefore raise each other. In other words, the world is unfair, but if you have it in your power to make it a little bit better for another human being, it is your moral duty to do so. You can make the world a better place.

"In my real estate business, I have the chance to do this in many ways, and you also have those chances every time you interact with people.

For example:

- When hiring people, always offer a fair wage.
- When screening new tenants, always keep the screening process and the rents fair.

- When paying for services, always pay on time and with appropriate compensation for a job well done.
- If someone is in need and you have the funds, then donate to their cause.

"Morality is simply doing the right thing. The right thing lifts people and improves their life. It is never wrong to err on the side of kindness. We can give others the benefit of the doubt, a smile, and when possible, a helping hand. My father would not have been able to grow up without his siblings carrying his books home from school. I couldn't have grown up without my father's lessons and my mother's strength of character. The world was unfair to them very often, but at the end of the day, they did their best to always do the right thing. They raised me to do the same, and it has shaped my entire life.

"Living a moral life can only ever serve to enhance the quality of that life. Doing the right thing for yourself will make you feel good, and doing the right thing by others can shape the lives of those others in a good way".

Chapter 3 Standout Points

❶ Cultural norms have changed. Respect for elders and those in authority has changed. News stories of police officers, nurses, and teachers having to deal with abusive behaviour are common, and in many areas, where once there was neighbourliness, politeness, and general kindness towards others in the local community, there is now hostility, rudeness, and no community spirit whatsoever. The question is, does it need to be this way?

❷ "It's not whether you win or lose, it's how you play the game". Standing out in life should be standing out for the right reasons.

❸ Becoming someone of strong moral character isn't something that happens by accident, it's something you need to intentionally do.

❹ The values you live your life by are *your* choice. Showing kindness to others is your choice; treating yourself and others with respect is your choice; caring for other people, and protecting the vulnerable is your choice, and so is *not* doing any of these things.

❺ Good morals are infectious. If you smile at someone, they'll often smile back at you in return. If you treat someone with kindness, they will often return that kindness, or extend it to someone else.

Chapter 4

How to Restore Morality in Society

Restoring morality may sound like a huge undertaking; perhaps so huge that you're left wondering if there's anything you can do that will make any kind of difference. Is there any point? Yes, there is. The really important thing to remember is that you're not responsible for the way everyone on Earth chooses to think and behave, you're only responsible for your own thoughts and actions...

"You must be the change you wish to see in the world".

This very famous quote is often attributed to Mahatma Gandhi. However, while the message in the words fits well with Gandhi's philosophy, there's no evidence to suggest he actually said them. In fact, they were written by Arleen Lorrance in her work known as The Love Project. During the 1960s and 70s, Arleen was a high school teacher in Brooklyn, New York. She was becoming increasingly aware of the violence and poverty her students were experiencing in their lives and decided to try to improve the situation through improving their education. She encouraged them to believe a better life was possible, and by practicing what she preached, she *showed* them how to make change happen for themselves.

Her philosophy was that if young people growing up in rough neighbourhoods experienced an oasis of calm and acceptance when they attended school, it would not only boost their potential to learn, but also positively impact their day-to-day lives. In effect, she created the change she wanted to see in the world by *being* that change in all she thought, said, and did. As more students began to change their lives for the better, the example they set in the way they thought and behaved then inspired others to think and behave in the same way. The Love Project was a success. Daily life in the school was transformed, and the ripple effect it created meant the positivity was soon carried out into the surrounding community by the students. All of Brooklyn benefited.

Societal "Rules"

You already know that not everyone shares the same morals, but there are certain rules in society that are necessary if people are to live together in any kind of harmony. Imagine if people chose to make up their own minds about which side of the road they should drive on, or whether to stop at a red light? Some rules just need to be laws that *everyone* must obey. But, what about the rules some choose to abide by and some don't? For example, picking up your dog's mess in a public space is law in many parts of the UK, but clearly not everyone abides by that law. The same applies to parking a vehicle on a pavement. It's not always illegal, but considering the fact that it blocks pedestrian access and causes a road hazard for other vehicles, shouldn't it be a common decency rule *not* to do it? What about parking in a disabled space when you're not a blue badge holder? This *is* against the law, but some people still choose to do it. What about queue-jumping? Not illegal, but does that make it okay to do it?

The point being highlighted here is that societal "rules" exist to create some sense of order and civility in daily life. Another way of thinking about this is to imagine trying to play a new board game or card game without any game rules to follow. You see, if everyone makes up their own rules, it becomes impossible to play the game. It's not unusual for young children to become upset when a game isn't going their way and they may try to change existing rules to ensure they win – perhaps insisting that landing on a snake in Snakes and Ladders doesn't mean sliding down the board, or at least not for them, only others! Well, unfortunately, some of those children continue to think and behave in a similar way as they grow into adults. Rules that don't suit them are disregarded – those rules only apply to other people. This selfish attitude filters into every aspect of life, and looking out for number one creates an environment of competition in just about everything, rather than one of cooperation.

Something not everyone is aware of is that it's illegal to take a pebble from a beach in the UK. This law applies to any natural material found on a beach, including sand and shells. Of course, not everyone abides by this law and their "doesn't-apply-to-me" attitude no doubt leads them to think along the lines of, "it's just one little pebble, what harm can it do?". The problem here is that if it's okay for them to take a pebble, then it's okay for everyone in the country to take a pebble, so it's okay for 67,000,000 pebbles to be removed from the beach.

This is *not* okay. In an attempt to manage Britain's eroding coastline, it had to become a criminal offence to remove even one pebble, and it's in *everyone's* interest to cooperate.

Each and every one of us *can* help to make the world a better place. Change *can* happen when each of us takes personal responsibility for the way we think and act. We're only responsible for our own thoughts and actions, but if we all do what we believe to be the right thing to do, the collective effort *will* make a difference.

A Cautionary Tale

If you are familiar with the story of *Lord of the Flies*, you'll be aware of the grim view of human nature it contains. Written by William Golding, and first published in 1954, it tells the story of a group of adolescent schoolboys trapped on a remote island after a plane crash. With no adult survivors, the boys need to fend for themselves. Initial efforts to work together for survival through elected leaders soon begin to unravel, and a vicious downward spiral into cruelty and chaos begins.

The author lived through WWII, and the plight of the boys reflects his observation that desperate times can bring out the worst in people. During the war, he noted that even well-educated, civilised, upstanding members of the community, such as doctors and lawyers, could still commit atrocities, leading him to question human nature. In *Lord of the Flies*, the boys' rapid descent into chaos when thrown into an environment without the usual rules and regulations that hold a civilised society together perhaps suggests that the author sees the same potential for any one of us to behave in the same way. A grim view of human nature indeed, but the thought-provoking tale has become a classic that children continue to study in school.

Be the Change

With this cautionary tale in mind, we're taken back to the need for societal "rules" to create some sense of order and civility in daily life. There will always be individuals with a selfish doesn't-apply-to-me attitude, but that doesn't mean there's no point in choosing to live your life by your own moral standards. You must be the change you wish to see in the world.

Think about all the situations you might find yourself facing on an average day, and the challenging ones that might bring out the worst in you in particular. Do you always think and behave as your best self? For example, have you ever found yourself feeling frustrated by people bumping into you on busy pavements or in crowded corridors? Perhaps it's the way they seem to rush around without giving any thought to the effect they're having on other people, or the way they seem to be so caught up in looking at their phones that they don't even acknowledge your existence, let alone apologise, that irks you? Well, take a moment to consider whether the annoyance of the situation has ever led to you behaving in the same way? If you're driving, have you ever found yourself getting mad at other drivers for failing to let you out at a busy junction?

Well, did running late as a consequence lead to you failing to let another driver out at the next junction?

Have you ever bought more of something than you needed at a supermarket because you've heard there may be a shortage? At the height of the Covid 19 pandemic in 2020, customers had to be rationed to one pack of toilet rolls per household to help cope with a shortage on the shelves that occurred purely through panic buying. Had everyone carried on buying their usual supply, the shelves would not have become empty. In reality, there was no shortage, it was nothing more than the result of selfish people filling their trolleys and their homes with more toilet rolls than they needed – because they'd heard there may be a shortage. Have you ever found yourself complaining bitterly about the traffic while you're stuck in a traffic jam? Well, if you're in your car, you *are* the traffic you're complaining about. If you want the congestion problem to be resolved, *you* need to change your habits. If you're not prepared to make a switch to public transport, why should anyone else? Complaining about the actions of other people won't change anything if you're doing exactly the same. Take a moment to reflect on the pebbles on the beach example!

Leo Tolstoy once said, "Everyone thinks of changing the world, but no one thinks of changing himself". Change needs to come from each one of us as individuals first. The success of The Love Project in the 1970s demonstrates that the actions of one person can ripple out and change the actions of many others, and that a collective effort *will* make a difference.

If you always strive to be your best and do your best, you become a positive influence on others. The key to making the world a better place is to keep striving to be better ourselves. If each one of us begins each new day with thoughts of being better than we were yesterday, we can positively influence the world around us, adding value to the lives of everyone in our communities.

Small Acts of Kindness that can make a Big Difference...

To demonstrate just how easy it is to brighten someone's day, here's a list of 25 small ways to make a big difference. Not all of them will apply to you and your circumstances, but you may be surprised by just how many you can put into action right away.

Hold the door open for someone: A tiny act of consideration for others that can raise a smile and brighten a day.

Pay for someone's coffee: Perhaps you've noticed someone in the queue looking like they could use a break, or maybe you happened to see them doing something nice for someone else. Even for no particular reason, paying for someone else's coffee can give both them and you a boost.

Compliment a stranger: Maybe they're wearing a fabulous pair of shoes; maybe they've just performed brilliantly in your exercise class; maybe they're responsible for a particularly well-behaved dog (or child!). Just say something nice where it's deserved.

Leave a note in a public place: You don't need to know who will read your note, you just need to know that you've left a positive message for someone to read. Who knows how much it may brighten their day?

Send a handwritten letter: In today's world of text messages and emails, a handwritten letter can make someone feel special.

Offer to help for free: Whether it's helping with child-minding, watering the plants, doing some housework, running an errand, or anything else, doing something to help out a neighbour brings its own reward in the form of community spirit. Even offering to help a stranger pack their groceries at a busy checkout or load them into their car can be a "life-saving" offer of help when they're perhaps struggling on their own or trying to deal with a toddler!

Share homemade treats: If you've baked up a batch of biscuits, why not take them into work and treat your co-workers? Or, if you grow things in your garden, why not spread the joy by sharing your produce with your neighbours?

Leave a gift for a neighbour: It's a sad fact that we often don't know who our neighbours are, let alone speak to them. This is often because life is hectic, and we rush out in the morning and home again in the evening. Leaving a small gift, or just a note to say "hello" on the doorstep can go a long way towards sparking friendships that build communities.

Volunteer at a local charity: Giving up even a small amount of free time to be a volunteer can make a huge difference to the running of an invaluable voluntary organisation. Getting involved in any type of volunteer role is good for your wellbeing. Helping others is known to create a feel-good factor that elevates your mood, and surrounding yourself with like-minded people who value the same cause is a morally elevating experience.

Donate to charity: Whether it's clothes to a clothes bank, books to a book bank, food to a food bank, blood to a blood bank, leftover paint to a community project, or any other form of donation, giving brightens so many other people's days.

Give someone a coin or trolley token at a supermarket: If you've ever been unable to access a supermarket trolley, you'll understand the difference this act of kindness can make in someone's day!

Share _only_ positive posts: You may be tempted to get into a social media argument with anyone who challenges your point of view, but you're unlikely to ever change anyone's mind. Instead, choose to post only positive comments about things that matter to you. It doesn't matter what someone else believes, it only matters what you believe, so share your passion, positivity, and hopefulness and you never know who you may influence.

Send flowers to a local care home: Brighten the day of care home residents and staff by sending a bunch of colourful blooms to display in the building.

Be a tutor or mentor: Put your skills and knowledge to good use by teaching or guiding others in your community. Use your passion to inspire others.

Give up your seat to someone who needs it: Whether it's a seat on a busy train or a seat in a crowded waiting room, this small act can make all the difference in someone else's day.

Be generous with your tips: If the service was good, make sure it's rewarded. Even if you're not in a position to be more generous with money, be generous in your praise. Everyone feels good when they feel valued.

Share your umbrella on a rainy day: If it's raining cats and dogs, why not invite the unprepared person getting soaked at the bus stop to share your umbrella?

Give up your place in a queue: This kind gesture is so uncommon it may take them by surprise, but letting someone jump in ahead of you when you're not in a hurry can really make their day.

Leave a positive review for a small business: Positive feedback can really help a small business to boost its profile. All too often, people only take the time to leave feedback when they have complaints. Choose to highlight the positives in your experience.

Show your appreciation for service providers: Whether it's the postman, the binmen, the street sweeper, the bus driver, or anyone else who provides a service in your neighbourhood, make sure you let them know that you appreciate them and what they do. Yes, it's their job, but everyone deserves credit for a job well done.

Offer to carpool with co-workers: Sharing a car can go a long way towards cutting congestion on the roads, but it could also make a huge difference to someone struggling with transport costs or public transport timetable challenges.

Offer to cook a meal for a busy friend: A home-cooked meal that's ready to eat could be a meal that makes a world of difference to a friend who is run off their feet.

Buy lunch for a co-worker: On a similar note to the above, popping out to buy lunch for a co-worker stuck at their desk with a mountain of work to get through could be a gesture that makes their day bearable.

Organise a community event: Whether it's a community clean-up, arranging the planting of flowers in a communal area, a picnic in the park, or anything else that the whole community can be invited to take part in, you can help to brighten the lives of everyone in your local area by showing that you care.

Be an active listener: Sometimes all it takes to lift someone's mood is to be heard. By simply taking the time to really listen to what someone has to say, you can make a big difference to their day... And perhaps even their life.

When you consider how much these small gestures may mean to someone else, you realise that all it takes to make the world a better place is to be kind in whatever way you can.

Cultivating Moral Resilience

This chapter began with a query over whether restoring morality in society may be just too huge an undertaking, and perhaps too big a task for any one individual to take on. You now know that you *can* make a difference, and we can all make the world a better place. However, that said, it's fair to add that there can be times when the thinking and behaviour of others leaves you feeling at a loss. Perhaps you feel the company you work for is not being managed ethically, or that your boss is putting profit before customer care. Perhaps you feel unable to do your job in the way you feel is right because your hands are tied with a lack of support and resources.

Feeling this way can leave you feeling powerless to change anything, and worst of all, it can leave you with an overwhelming feeling of having to compromise yourself and what you believe in, day in and day out. It's a feeling now known as "moral distress", a term coined in the early 1980s by a philosopher named Andrew Jameton. At the time, he used it to describe what was happening to nurses on the wards, constantly finding themselves facing systemic or institutional barriers that prevented them from doing the right thing by every patient. Sadly, moral distress remains high in the nursing profession, but the concept has broadened across many other professions, including all medical professionals, emergency service providers, law enforcement, teachers, social service providers – and any other environment where an individual is left feeling that forces outside of their control are causing them to repeatedly comprise something they value.

Anyone facing a day-to-day environment in which their values aren't respected may suffer moral distress. Feelings of frustration and anger are likely to grow when someone feels restricted or devalued, and the outcome will often be exhaustion, burnout, and eventually disconnection. All of this can lead to "compassion fatigue" or diminished moral sensitivity, meaning an ongoing sense of being powerless to change anything.

If you find yourself feeling powerless, or struggling to hold on to your integrity, there are steps you can take to build moral resilience.

Develop Self-Awareness: Get to the heart of who you really are and what you believe in. You need to know what truly matters to you to know when your integrity is being compromised. The greater your self-awareness, the more open you become to acknowledging your strengths, weaknesses, and potential biases. This makes room for exploring where change in you may inspire change in others, and it paves the way to dealing with morally challenging situations in a way that allows you to hold your head high.

Learn to Self-regulate: You can't control what other people think and do, but you can be the master of your own mind and body. Learning to self-regulate is learning to accept that you can't control every situation, but you can control how you react and respond to any situation. Self-regulation is self-mastery, and with this mastery you give yourself the best opportunity to find a way around challenges without compromising your values.

Choose to Express Yourself: In choosing to express yourself, you choose to voice your concerns about moral issues. This doesn't mean forcing your beliefs on others, it simply means creating an opportunity for discussion, and thereby an opportunity to gain a greater understanding of different points of view.

Create Meaning: There can be times when you question if anything you do makes any difference? This is especially so when you're facing a moral challenge. You might ask yourself, *why am I still doing this when nothing ever changes?* or, *what is the point of this when nothing I do will ever be enough?* By creating meaning, you're not attempting to put a rose-tinted positive spin on things, but you are looking for the very real benefits of continuing to do what you do. Those benefits are there when you choose to look for them, and it's recognising them that allows you to keep moving forward with integrity.

Engage with Others: Research has concluded that connecting with others is a basic human need, and experiments have shown that our brains "light up" when we talk to others, allowing us to mimic the behaviours and emotions of the speaker. Talking to and connecting with trusted others is an extremely important part of building moral resilience. The saying goes that a problem shared is a problem halved, and simply knowing that you are not alone in your moral struggle can go a long way towards alleviating a sense of isolation and despair.

Moral Elevation

Sarina Saturn, a researcher at the University of Portland, has said, "Moral elevation not only boosts our positive emotions, but it also promotes our love for our fellow human and inspires us to be better people. Indeed, making an effort to experience more moral elevation will restore our faith in humanity and encourage us to help other people". This sounds like something we need to restore morality in society, so what exactly is moral elevation? The answer to this question may surprise you. Moral elevation is simply the lift you feel in your mood, or the warm feeling you get when you see someone do something good for someone else. In particular, morally courageous things such as rescuing strangers or defenceless animals from perilous situations, or giving up lucrative careers to give more time to greater causes.

Research has also revealed that witnessing acts of kindness can motivate us to take better care of ourselves. Seeing the good in others can inspire us to be good to ourselves as well as others, with one study finding that depressed individuals chose to seek treatment after experiencing moral elevation. This suggests that seeking good news stories may have an important role to play in maintaining a sense of hope in a world that sometimes feels hopeless.

The Late, Great, Robin Williams

Before his death in 2014, the world knew Robin Williams as a larger-than-life actor and comedian. What wasn't so well known was just how kind he was throughout his career, and how much he did for other people without any desire for publicity or personal gain. He was involved with many charities, including Comic Relief and St Jude's Children's Research Hospital, and he regularly visited American troops in Iraq and Afghanistan to thank them for their service. However, he also stood up for those who very often couldn't stand up for themselves. Whenever he worked on a movie or took part in an event, he requested that the hiring company must also hire a certain number of homeless people in the area and give them work, and when working with young actors on a movie, he would step in whenever necessary to protect them from working extra hours. But perhaps the most touching stories of all have come from ordinary people who discovered Robin's kindness in the most unexpected of places. One such story tells of a grieving family on their way home from a memorial service being approached by him. He didn't approach them as a celebrity, he was simply a kind-hearted stranger wishing to lift their spirits in any small way he could. In another, he approached a woman travelling alone in an airport after he witnessed her becoming stressed and emotional during check in. Once again, he didn't approach her as a celebrity, he simply approached to ask if she was okay.

Another story of Robin's kindness was told by fellow actor Christopher Reeve. After the riding accident that left him paralysed, Christopher recalls being in his hospital bed when Robin burst through the door wearing scrubs and announced in a Russian accent that he was a proctologist and needed to examine him immediately. He said this became the first time he'd laughed since the accident, and from that moment on he knew life was going to be okay.

"Everyone you meet is fighting a battle you know nothing about. Be kind. Always" – Robin Williams.

George Michael

Another star whose kindness and generosity only became known after his death is George Michael. After his death in 2016, stories began to emerge of him working undercover in homeless shelters, paying stranger's debts, and funding one woman's IVF treatment. He did everything in secret, and he wanted it kept that way. These gestures were not publicity stunts, they were genuine acts of kindness.

A contestant appearing on *Deal or No Deal* revealed that she was taking part in the hope of winning enough money to fund her IVF treatment. She didn't win the money, but George was watching the programme and called the show afterwards to donate the £15,000 she needed. The donation was made secretly, and the woman didn't discover it had been made by George until after his death.

According to another revelation, George was having coffee in a café one day when he overheard a woman crying as she spoke to her friend about mounting debts.

He proceeded to write a cheque for £25,000 and asked the waitress to give it to the woman – but only after he had left.

Clearly a generous man, George not only provided monetary support where he could, he also gave his time to support causes he cared about. For many years, he had worked at a homeless shelter, but he did so anonymously, asking his work colleagues to keep it secret. It was only after his death that they told the story, saying, 'He asked that we never told anyone. That's who he was.'

Kind and generous is who he was, not who he *pretended* to be or wanted to be seen as. He didn't need anyone to know. Knowing that he was living his life by his values was all that mattered. In 2006, he gave a free concert just for nurses. It took place at the Camden Roundhouse in London, and before taking to the stage, he said, 'Almost 10 years ago, during the last week of my mother's life, I told my friends and family that if I ever played my own concerts again, I would make sure to do a free one for NHS nurses. The nurses that helped my family at that time were incredible people, and I realised just how undervalued these amazing people are. So I want to thank them with a Christmas concert.'

One nurse who was there remembers it fondly. She says, 'A nervous George Michael took to the stage with a bad cold and told us he'd played in front of crowds all over the world but was anxious because he'd never performed in front of so many heroes before. He will always be a hero to all of the nurses at the Roundhouse that night.'

Another story tells of George being a "hero" as he came to the rescue of a woman with a flat tyre. A woman remembers leaving her work in the early 1990s and discovering she had a flat tyre. She says, 'I was working on Edgware Road in London near the Sony Studios. I came out of work to find my little 1974 Ford Fiesta had a flat tyre. George Michael was coming out of Sony as I was standing there in the rain and helped me change my tyre... I've never forgotten how kind he was.'

It's perhaps worth noting that these events took place before the days of social media. In today's world, such encounters with the general public are perhaps unlikely to remain secret for long! However, anonymity was what George requested, and the fact that his request was respected until after his death speaks volumes about the sort of man he was.

"You'll never find peace of mind until you listen to your heart" – George Michael.

What we can take away from these celebrity stories is that you can't change the world on your own, but you can change your corner of it, and the ripple effect will expand your reach. Moral elevation helps you to stand by your moral values and always do what you know to be the right thing to do.

Finding your own moral elevation

Look for good news stories: Newspapers focus on stories of doom and gloom. It's an inescapable fact that the most sensational news is news that sells, so broaden your horizons and choose to consume different types of media. There are good news stories out there every day, but you may need to be proactive in your approach. Try googling "heart-warming stories" or "random acts of kindness" and you may be surprised by just how many you find.

Practice mindfulness: Mindfulness is being fully present in the moment. It's all too easy to let worries about what's happening in the world at large get in the way of experiencing what's happening in *your* world. Getting caught up in stress and negativity prevents you from seeing and experiencing the positive things in your life, so take time in your day to be fully present in the here and now, and notice the beauty that surrounds you.

Develop a moral elevation habit: If you're in the habit of checking your emails or the news headlines first thing every morning, why not change this potentially mood-crushing start to your day and choose to elevate your mood with something much more positive instead. Get into the habit of doing something you enjoy every morning, whether it's exercising, meditating, reading good news stories, a few more pages of a novel, or anything else. If you start your day in a way that makes you feel good, you're going to take that positive mood with you into your day and out to everyone you connect with. Moral elevation is contagious!

Chapter 4 Standout Points

❶ You are not responsible for the way everyone on Earth chooses to think and behave, you're only responsible for your own thoughts and actions... "You must be the change you wish to see in the world".

❷ Each and every one of us *can* help to make the world a better place. Change *can* happen when each of us takes personal responsibility for the way we think and act.

❸ There will always be individuals with a selfish doesn't-apply-to-me attitude, but that doesn't mean there's no point in choosing to live your life by your own moral standards.

❹ You can't change the world on your own, but you can change your corner of it, and the ripple effect will expand your reach.

❺ The key to making the world a better place is to keep striving to be better ourselves.

Chapter 5

How to Build Good Character with High Moral Standards

It's time to reflect on the information presented in the previous chapters, and to consider not only what it means to have good character, but also how to build it. Being someone of good character with high moral standards is standing out for the right reasons in life. It's all about who you are and how you present yourself in what you do; it's being your best, but not in terms of striving for perfection, only striving to be the best *you* can be.

The positive character traits that allow us to be and do our best in all aspects of life include honesty, authenticity, integrity, responsibility, respectfulness, humility, and perseverance. In this chapter, we take a look at ways to develop these traits, and delve a little deeper into the positive benefits they bring.

Ways to Build Good Character

Be True to Yourself – Your Best Self

To be true to yourself, you need to know who you are. This takes us back to the importance of morals and values, and getting clear on what matters most to you. What do you truly value? Once you're clear on who you are, and perhaps most importantly, who you *want* to be, you now need an element of self-discipline to ensure you always think and behave as this version of you. This is especially important when facing choices in day-to-day life. Let's face it, if one of the options available to you is the "easy" one, you're likely to take it, but which option represents the right choice? Which option is aligned with you as your best self, and your values and goals in life? Having good character and high moral standards means doing the right thing, and the right thing isn't always the easy option.

For example, let's say you find yourself with a choice of project to take on in your workplace. One of them would take only a matter of hours to complete because you've done plenty of others just like it, but the other one involves new instructions and a different approach. Clearly, the first option represents the easy option, but the second option represents an opportunity to grow your skills and expand your thinking. You see, the *right* choice for you is the one that aligns with the best version of you. The more you push yourself, the more you grow.

"You change the world by being yourself" – Yoko Ono.

The story of Rosa Parks serves to demonstrate the power of sticking firmly to beliefs, no matter how many difficulties this choice may bring. Her decision not to take the easy option of leaving her seat in the bus led to her becoming a well-respected figurehead of the American civil rights movement.

Spend Time with Positive Role Models

Following on from the above, one of the most effective ways to help maintain self-discipline is to surround yourself with people who already demonstrate the qualities you aspire to have. If you spend time with positive people, their positivity rubs off on you. If you spend time with people who always choose the opportunity to grow over the easy option, their disciplined attitude rubs off on you. If you spend time with people you admire for any reason, the qualities that make them admirable in your eyes rub off on you. Whatever it is you respect and admire in others can become something others recognise in you when you choose to immerse yourself in an environment that encourages you to be and do better.

"You are the average of the five people you spend the most time with" – Jim Rohn.

There have been many successful mentor-mentee relationships throughout history. Talk show star, Oprah Winfrey, was mentored by celebrated author and poet, Maya Angelou. She says, 'Maya was there for me always, guiding me through some of the most important years of my life. Mentors are important and I don't think anybody makes it in the world without some form of mentorship.'

Put Yourself Out There – Take Risks

One quality you may admire in others is the ability to take on challenges without fearing failure. Being able to put yourself out there and take risks doesn't mean being reckless in your actions, it means being able to adopt a "nothing ventured, nothing gained" attitude and choosing to try new and challenging things rather than shy away from them. Character is built through facing fears and coming out the other side – win or lose. As the saying goes, "You can't win 'em all", but you certainly can't win if you don't put yourself on the start line! With the right attitude, failure isn't losing, it's gaining experience and knowledge that allows you to be and do better next time. You don't need to fail every time before you can succeed, but if you've never experienced failure, you've probably never challenged yourself to be more than you are. Every challenge offers new opportunities to learn, so try, don't be shy, and switch, what-if-I-fail-thinking to, what-if-I-succeed-thinking instead. What have you got to lose when you consider all you have to gain? You'll find there are always positives to be found in every outcome.

"I believe that the most important single thing, beyond discipline and creativity, is daring to dare" – Maya Angelou.

When Amelia Earhart dared to be flown across the Atlantic, she dared to do something no woman had done before her. In 1928, she dared to fly solo across the North American continent – and back. She made history as the first woman to achieve this, and then dared to become the first woman to fly solo nonstop across the Atlantic. She once said, "The most difficult thing is the decision to act; the rest is merely tenacity. The fears are paper tigers. You can do anything you decide to do. You can act to change and control your life; and the procedure, the process, is its own reward".

Step Outside your Comfort Zone

To be able to put yourself out there, you need to step out of your comfort zone. Your comfort zone is a non-challenging place where you feel totally at ease, and while it's a good place to be from time to time while you take stock of all you've achieved to get there, it's not somewhere you should choose to stay. Remember, if you're not pushing yourself, you're not growing. As many wise people have said, if you want to get to the next level, you need get comfortable with being uncomfortable. Being uncomfortable simply means doing something you don't necessarily know how to do; it's trying new things, or doing things differently, and therefore it's putting yourself out there in a challenging situation where failure is a possibility.

You don't need to take a giant leap out of comfort zone, you can begin with just small steps. For example, if you always eat the same thing for breakfast every morning, try something totally different. If you always take the same route to and from work without any variation, try venturing down an alternative route and see where it takes you. Every new or different thing you do offers opportunities to learn and grow. Perhaps you might take a bigger step out of your comfort zone by signing up for a volunteer job in an environment that's different to the norm for you, or join a class to learn something you've never had the courage to do – even though you'd like to be able to do it. In the words of Eleanor Roosevelt, "Do something every day that scares you. You have nothing to lose but fear itself".

"Just try new things. Don't be afraid. Step out of your comfort zones and soar" – Michelle Obama.

Learn to Recognise and Embrace your Defining Moments

The moments in life in which you feel challenged are defining moments. Challenges can be mental or physical, but they are those moments in which you feel tested. Learning to recognise these defining moments helps you to learn from them and grow through the experience gained – whatever the outcome.

For example, you might be able to think of a time when you tried something and failed. How did you react? Did you give up; did you get angry with yourself; did you take it on the chin and try again? With the benefit of hindsight, was your response the best one? What would you choose to do differently if you were in the same situation again? In learning to recognise these defining moments, you learn to understand your choices. Failures will happen, mistakes will be made, but your response to these happenings is always your choice. Remember, where there's a challenge, there's an opportunity to learn.

"If you don't go after what you want, you'll never have it. If you don't ask, the answer is always no. If you don't step forward, you're always in the same place" – Nora Roberts.

Learn to Manage your Emotions

With the benefit of hindsight, you may come to realise that your emotional responses to past happenings were not the most helpful. When you take a moment to consider how you have typically reacted to things *not* going to plan, you may begin to notice a pattern. For example, if wallowing in self-pity is something you tend to do, has it ever been helpful? Or, if you tend to get angry and take it out on other people, has this approach ever been helpful? Paying attention to your emotions and the reactions they create can help you to gain a clearer understanding of which thoughts and behaviours have been helpful and which have ultimately held you back and prevented you from finding the positives in a tough situation. Upsets and setbacks are inevitable, but character is built on your attitude to them and how you choose to handle them.

"Your attitude, not your aptitude, will determine your altitude" – Zig Ziglar.

Be Gracious in Defeat

In the game of life, it's an inescapable fact that you'll win some and you'll lose some. Being a success, or being your best, is not dependant on winning. Understanding this makes it easier to be gracious in defeat, and to accept that failing at something does not make *you* a failure.

Remember that game of Snakes and Ladders you lost? Instead of trying to change the rules, choose to change the way you lose. Learn to accept losing as nothing more than learning, and use every setback as an opportunity to grow wiser and better prepared for next time. If you can be gracious in defeat in a board game, you can be gracious in defeat in all other areas of life. However, it's also important to note that good character is not only shown in being a good loser, but also in being a good winner – steer clear of bragging!

"Learn to be a gracious winner and an outstanding loser" – Joe Namath.

Stay Humble – and Be Kind

In other words, try to be nice. It's fair to say that the world isn't always a kind place, but this doesn't mean you can't make a difference in your little corner by spreading kindness in all you say and do. The good energy you put out into the world around you will be returned to you, and, as the saying goes, one good deed deserves another. In showing kindness and understanding in the way you interact with someone, they are much more likely to return the favour or show the same kindness and consideration in the way they interact with someone else.

Empathising with others and being supportive is character building. Broadening your horizons by interacting with people from all walks of life is a positive way to learn how to see another's perspective, and to avoid being judgemental. This doesn't mean you need to agree with everyone else's point of view, you simply learn how to see the world from another's perspective. Being able to empathise with others makes you approachable and trustworthy, and these character traits stand you in good stead to be the best you can be in all you say and do. Abraham Lincoln is a great example of the power of empathy. He always treated others, even his enemies, with patience and kindness, an attitude he summed up by saying, "I don't like that man. I must get to know him better".

"If a man be gracious and courteous to strangers, it shows he is a citizen of the world" – Francis Bacon.

Work on your Communication Skills

Good communication isn't just talking, it's also listening, but even more importantly, it's paying attention to what's being said. Characterful people are able to make conversation with everyone and anyone, even complete strangers. They know that having a friendly word to say can be all it takes to brighten someone's day, and they also know that there's always something to be learned from other people.

"To effectively communicate, we must realise that we are all different in the way we perceive the world and use this understanding as a guide to our communication with others" – Tony Robbins.

Be a Doer, not just a Talker

Good conversation skills make you approachable, as well as open to learning from others, but to really grow your character, you need to be prepared to put your words into action. This is especially important if you want to be considered a genuine person. To be authentic, what you say must match what you do. People very quickly spot discrepancies, and no one likes a fake.

To be the best version of you, you need to be your best in all you *do* – not just what you say you're going to do!

Get into the habit of being a doer by adopting a positive daily routine. Make a to-do list for each day, and then check everything off your list as it gets done. The aim is to complete your list by the end of the day so make sure it's manageable. If your to-do list slips into becoming a still-to-be-done list the next day, you're in danger of becoming a talker, not a doer. Break bigger tasks down into more manageable steps, and then tackle each step one day at a time.

"The world needs dreamers, and the world needs doers. But above all, the world needs dreamers who do" – Sarah Ban Breathnach.

Be Supportive

Building good character helps to build a good reputation, and your reputation can make or break your potential to succeed. However, a person of good character isn't only concerned with their own success, they are supportive of other people. With good character, a question you will always ask yourself is, *what can I do to help?* Little things can make a big difference, so build character by being supportive of other people in whatever way you can – no matter how small the gesture may seem.

Remember, becoming someone of strong moral character isn't something that happens by accident, it's something you need to intentionally do. This takes us back to questioning how intentionally kind and supportive you are in everyday life. Do you always give up your seat on crowded public transport, or does it depend on how you judge the people around you? In other words, are you always kind, or are you only kind when it's convenient?

"Do your little bit of good where you are; it's those little bits of good put together that overwhelm the world" – Desmond Tutu.

Challenge Yourself – Lead by Example

Setting yourself challenging (but manageable) goals is one way to challenge yourself to be and do better. Challenges can be mental or physical, but setting yourself targets that stretch you just a little closer to where you want to be and who you want to be will keep you on track to becoming your best. Take on tasks that take you out of your comfort zone; volunteer to help others complete projects they're struggling with; learn something completely new; and inspire others to do the same by adopting a positive attitude in all you do – even when you're not "winning"! Challenging yourself and others to be better requires commitment, and taking responsibility for your actions builds character.

"My biggest motivation? Just to keep challenging myself" – Sir Richard Branson.

Define your Goals – Dream Big

There's nothing quite like identifying a dream and going after it when it comes to building character. No matter what your goal or goals in life, the road to achieving it is not guaranteed to be a smooth one. Setbacks and failures are the bumps and roadblocks you encounter on your journey, but character is built in finding your way through or around those obstacles. As Walt Disney once said, "All our dreams can come true if we have the courage to pursue them". Pursuing a goal takes courage, commitment, and a can-do attitude. These are positive character traits we should all aspire to develop.

Take time to write down your goals. Some will be short-term goals and others long-term, but by simply writing them down, you begin the process of turning dreams into realities. A dream written down becomes a goal, and a goal can be achieved with a step-by-step action plan. Motivational speaker Mark Victor Hansen perhaps said it best when he said, "By recording your dreams and goals on paper, you set in motion the process of becoming the person you most want to be. Put your future in good hands – your own".

"Top people have very clear goals. They know who they are, and they know what they want. They write it down and they make plans for its accomplishment" – Brian Tracy.

Make your own Decisions

When you know who you are and who you want to be, you're in a much stronger position to make good decisions and choices in life. Not every decision you make will turn out to be the "best" in terms of eventual outcomes, but with strong character, you know that each decision you make represents the best choice for you at that moment in time, and each new moment brings new choices. There are no "good" or "bad" choices, only choices to be made, and as you know, there isn't always a clear right or wrong response in every situation, it comes down to your character and your values. However, are you taking responsibility for your choices, or are you handing responsibility for outcomes to "luck" or "fate"? When you have defined your goals and identified your purpose, you know what you need to do to make your own luck and decide your own fate. Making your own choices is a key element of developing character, and the stronger your character, the more you take control of your life. Remember, the things you value and the principles you stand by in life help to influence your every decision, motivating you to do the right thing.

"Do you wait for things to happen, or do you make them happen yourself? I believe in writing your own story" – Charlotte Eriksson.

Be Better Today than you were Yesterday

Building character isn't an overnight process. When you take all of the above into consideration, you realise there's no magic wand that can be waved to instantly develop good character. *Your* character is only ever as strong as *your* core values and beliefs; your character is who you are, and it's what you do, not just what you say. Building good character takes consistency and authenticity in your every thought and action, and it requires a commitment to being and doing your best.

Whatever it is you want to change or improve, begin by creating a clear picture in your mind of what it looks like when you've achieved it. Next, make a plan that takes you from where you are to where you want to be, and then take one step at a time to get there. For example, perhaps you want to improve your communication skills. Instead of trying to take a giant leap from where you are, make the first step more manageable by focusing only on being a better listener, and then the next step can be improving your conversation skills by trying out interesting questions. Put the two together and you have improved your communication skills.

To be the best you can be, use each new day as an opportunity to be just that little bit better than the previous day. It's not about being "the best" or being the winner, it's simply being all you can be – one step and one day at a time.

"The goal is not to be perfect by the end. The goal is to be better today" – Simon Sinek.

Chapter 5 Standout Points

❶ Having good character and high moral standards means doing the right thing, and the right thing isn't always the easy option.

❷ The *right* choice for you is the one that aligns with the best version of you. The more you push yourself, the more you grow.

❸ Surround yourself with people who already demonstrate the qualities you aspire to have. Whatever it is you respect and admire in others can become something others recognise in you when you choose to immerse yourself in an environment that encourages you to be and do better.

❹ To be the best you can be, use each new day as an opportunity to be just that little bit better than the previous day. It's not about being "the best" or being the winner, it's simply being all you can be – one step and one day at a time.

Chapter 6

Benefits of Building Good Character with High Moral Standards

Modern life is full of pressures to think a certain way, be a certain way, and do a certain way. Social media constantly promotes the latest trends, and everyone posts "best-life" images for all to see. It's no surprise that being bombarded with these images and influences can make it difficult to be yourself. You feel almost forced into being someone you're not just to fit in, and the fear of missing out is ever-present if your life doesn't match up to #livingthebestlife ideals!

The really crucial thing to realise here is that what you see and read is not necessarily real. Perhaps some of those "best-life" images are genuine, but are they telling the whole story? It's fair to suspect not. Are the ordinary days or the bad days included alongside the best days? Not usually. Are the setbacks and disappointments mentioned? Not unless they're hugely dramatic or hilarious. The sad reality is that being *real* doesn't make you interesting, cool, hip, trendy, or noticeable in any other way – you don't attract followers. Without followers, you can't sell or promote whatever it is you're making money out of, and you can't achieve fame. Even more sad is the fact that any type of notoriety can be claimed as "fame" – leading to fortune – because being someone everyone loves to hate still counts as being popular!

Take a moment to consider how many so-called reality TV stars or social media influencers are *genuinely* the person they promote themselves to be. Now consider how many of them are promoting a manufactured image. How can pretending to be someone you're not ever be considered living your best life? And, how can striving to emulate a successful influencer who is in fact living a lie ever lead to anything *real* or lasting for all those followers?

Actress Judy Garland once said, "Always be a first-rate version of yourself; not a second-rate version of someone else". It's perhaps human nature to compare ourselves to others, but there's nothing to be gained from trying to achieve an unrealistic goal that's based on something entirely fake.

The benefit of building good character with high moral standards is that you become someone who has what it takes to *always* remain true to yourself...

You have true integrity: No matter what the latest trends, you will never compromise who you are and what you value. This is not to say you're unwilling to compromise on other things, you're just not prepared to be anything other than your authentic self – even if it means not "fitting in" at times. You stick by your values, and you follow your own path.

"Be honestly and unapologetically you. Because you being uniquely you will allow the people you interact with to feel comfortable being uniquely them – perhaps for the first time in their lives. There is no more authentic way to connect and no greater gift to give" – Scott Dinsmore.

You keep your word: You stick by your commitments, and you can be relied upon to keep your promises because keeping your word matters. The things you commit to doing are things you care about, and you care about getting them done.

You say what you mean and mean what you say: You don't say things just to curry favour with others. What you say is what you mean, and what you mean is always what matters most to you. Being authentic and staying true to your values is always more important than being "popular" or fitting in.

Morality is not just words, it's actions. What you say matches what you do, and actions often speak louder than words. Being honest and speaking the truth is important, but you're also prepared to roll up your sleeves and stand up for what you believe is right. This might mean joining a protest, signing a petition, or giving your time to support a worthy cause. What you say is what you mean, and what you mean is demonstrated in what you do.

You take responsibility for your actions: You are not afraid to own up to mistakes. Everyone makes mistakes, but not everyone is able to accept responsibility for their part in things not going to plan. You choose to learn from mistakes, rather than look for ways to pass the blame onto others, and you look for solutions rather than sweeping problems under the carpet in the hope of them not being noticed.

The story of Emily, a loan officer employed in a bank, provides a work-based example of this. Having just accepted a new position in the bank, she is mentored for the first month by a manager experienced in the same role. In the second month, she meets with her mentor to discuss a new loan application. Believing this to be an application that would be worked on together as a team, she gathers information and then files the application away for her manager to complete. Having moved on to other tasks, it takes two weeks before she discovers the loan application remains as she left it. It had not been sent to the underwriter for approval, so it had not been a team effort. Emily was entirely responsible for its completion.

Realising her mistake leaves Emily feeling embarrassed, but she chooses to own up to it immediately and explain the situation to her manager, rather than try to hide her error. Needless to say her manager isn't happy, but Emily's honesty allows the fastest solution to be found, and any further delay in the process avoided. Learning from her mistake, she is now clear on her responsibilities, and her actions in terms of taking responsibility for her error are valued by her manager.

You lend a hand whenever you can: You know that helping others to feel happy is the quickest route to boosting your own happiness. You genuinely care about other people, and you're always ready to lend a hand in any small way you can. From volunteering in an organisation to simply holding a door open for someone, doing what you can to help another human being really matters to you.

You treat everyone with respect: In your eyes, we are all equal in this world. You treat everyone you meet with the same level of respect, irrespective of differences in culture or opinion, and you remain open to different points of view. You earn respect by giving respect.

It's often said that you can tell a lot about someone by the way they treat waiters or shop assistants. If you're on a first date, for example, and the person you're with is rude and disrespectful to the waiter at your table, it should act as a red flag to who they *really* are – even if they're busy telling you about the work they like to do for charity! There's never a shortage of news stories about celebrities being rude to "little people" and actor James Cordon became one of them. After his astonishingly disrespectful behaviour towards waiting staff on more than one occasion, the restaurant owner used social media to name and shame him, stating that he was banned from returning. The ban was overturned after James apologised profusely, but I think it remains fair to question how genuine that apology was. Would he have apologised had it been the staff member who took to social media? Did he apologise and *mean* it, having realised the error of his ways, or did he simply apologise to ensure the restaurant ban was lifted – therefore for his own gain? You decide.

You don't try too hard to be liked: Everyone matters, but other people's opinions of you don't matter.

You don't need to be validated by others to feel good about who you are, and you know that by being true to yourself, the people you need to help you become the best you can be will be attracted into your life. Who chooses to like or dislike you is not your concern.

This takes us back to social media and the desperation of so many people to be "liked" and followed. Whether it's TikTok, Snapchat, Facebook, Instagram, X, or YouTube, these platforms are where popularity, or at least notoriety, are sought. Of course, the problem with this is that "fame" can be found without much effort – or, indeed, without any talent at all! How many famous people can you think of who are famous for being famous? Social media has made it easy to become known across multiple platforms and therefore known to just about the whole population. Posting a video that goes viral can be all it takes to launch an online influencer career. From there, the influencer can venture into a music career, or launch their own clothing brand, or produce their own fragrances, or publish a series of books, or star in their own fitness workouts... the list goes on. These "careers" are not the issue, it's the attempt to be relevant in *all* of them that's the problem. Is there anything original, unique, or even authentic in anything you do if you're just trying to be all things to all people?

Contestants on reality TV shows, for example, don't need to win to be able to gain from the experience. Any prize on offer is often secondary to the exposure gained and the opportunities this brings. The more platforms they can get across and the more products they can endorse, the more money they can make. The question that needs to be asked is whether any of what they say and do is congruent with who they really are and what they really believe. Instead of finding and sticking with a platform that fits with their personality and their values, they try to spread themselves across every available platform in *any* way possible. The quality of what they do, let alone the authenticity of it, appears to be immaterial. Being liked, being famous, and being wealthy appears to be of greater importance than being themselves – and who they truly believe themselves to be.

Back in 2007, *Keeping Up with the Kardashians* first aired on TV. The reality TV show ran for 20 series over almost 14 years, despite being panned from the outset by almost every critic. Whether viewers loved it or loathed it, they kept watching it, and it even won some audience awards. Each episode revolved around dysfunctional family drama and controversy, yet the viewers' ongoing interest in all of it allowed an already wealthy family to become even richer. Perhaps this goes to show that it's ordinary viewers who turn far-from-remarkable people into "celebrities" who are famous for being famous – nothing more. With this being the case, are we creating a culture that rewards unhealthy self-interest and narcissism? Is the desperation to be liked preventing us from discovering all we could be in life if we followed our own hearts and chose to walk our own path instead? Is being popular *really* of greater value than being true to yourself and your values?

The Emperor and the Seeds

There's an old tale that helps to demonstrate the power of knowing who you are and *always* remaining true to yourself in all you think and do. It's called *The Emperor and the Seeds*.

Long ago, the emperor of a kingdom gathered all the youths from across his lands into the palace. He gave each of them a pot with a seed planted in it and proclaimed, 'One day, one of you will replace me as emperor. Whoever can grow their seed to the greatest height in a year will become my successor.'

One of those boys took his pot home in great excitement. He couldn't wait to watch his seed grow, but after several weeks of watering it and tending to it carefully, there was nothing to be seen in his pot. He tried to ease his worries by considering that it might be a slow-growing seed and he just needed to be patient, but the weeks turned into months, and the one-year mark soon came around. The boy was full of worry – he had nothing but an empty pot to show the emperor.

On arrival at the palace, his fears became embarrassment as he saw that everyone else had beautifully tall plants in their pots. Other boys laughed and pointed at him, so he tried to hide himself at the back of the crowd to avoid any more unwanted attention.

The emperor looked at all the plants being presented to him, and then, just as the presentation was coming to an end, he saw the boy at the back. 'Come forward,' he said, gesturing, before announcing, 'you will be the new emperor.' Everyone in the crowd gasped. How could this be?

It transpired that the emperor had placed a boiled seed in each of the pots, meaning nothing could grow from any of them. Those who presented tall plants had clearly cheated and replaced the seed with another. Only the boy with the empty pot had remained honest, even when it meant being shown to be a "failure" in front of everyone else.

The moral of the tale is that an honest failure will always be rewarded over a dishonest success. Dishonesty will always be found out, so never sacrifice your integrity for the sake of appearances. In other words, don't be a sell-out!

Defy Expectation

Another benefit of always being who you know yourself to be as your best self – not who others believe you to be – is that you can defy expectation. A recent good-news story concerning some teenagers demonstrates this point beautifully. How many times do teenagers get a bad press? That's most of the time, right? We're conditioned to believe that teenagers are either layabouts or troublemakers, and thinking of anyone other than themselves is definitely *not* the expectation.

However, three teenage schoolboys defied expectation when they came to the rescue of a younger schoolboy. It was the first day of school after the summer break and the 11-year-old found himself on the wrong bus at the end of the day. He realised he was travelling in the wrong direction, and he didn't have a phone to contact his mum. Noticing the boy looking lost and upset, one of the teenagers approached to ask if he was okay. On discovering what had happened, the older boy instantly gave him £10 to get a taxi home. This was kind-hearted enough, but two other teenage boys then googled the number for a local taxi firm and suggested he should arrange to be picked up from outside one of their homes to make sure he was collected safely. The boys walked with him from the bus and waited to make sure the taxi arrived.

When the young boy's mum heard what had happened, she said it had restored her faith in humanity. The parents of the helpful teenagers felt extremely proud of their boys, and the boys themselves were pleased that teenagers were getting some good press for a change when the story was shared on Facebook.

The head teacher at the boys' school commented that such a lovely example had been set by the actions of the teenagers, and in a further addition to the good news story, it transpires that the taxi driver hadn't charged the boy for his ride home – perhaps another expectation defied!

When you have Strong Moral Character...

You don't have a big ego: A big ego is not a positive character trait, and it stands in the way of developing high moral standards. We all have an ego, and we might all get a little defensive from time to time when our pride is in danger of being hurt, but a big ego left unchecked becomes a much bigger problem. A big ego can lead to always needing to be in the limelight, always needing to be right, and always bragging about everything. This might sound like a strong and confident character, but it's most likely the opposite. Those with big egos are often the most insecure, and often feel threatened by others. A big ego generally goes hand-in-hand with self-centredness, and selfish behaviour is unlikely to be high moral behaviour.

With high moral standards, you value others every bit as much as you value yourself. You're a team player, and you look beyond your own needs to consider the needs of others. You don't base decisions purely on what *you* stand to gain or lose, you also consider the impact your actions may have on other people. You have the strength of character to look beyond yourself, and you have the inner strength to keep your ego in check – meaning no temper tantrums or diva behaviour when things are not going your way!

You are thoughtful and introspective: Thoughtfulness tends to inspire high moral standards. A thoughtful person will always take the needs of others into consideration, not just their own, but they will also tend to be self-reflective.

You already know that morals and values are influenced by many factors, and what you consider to be right and wrong may be very different to someone else's point of view. Morals evolve, and this is where an introspective approach becomes important. Unless you are able to reflect on your beliefs and opinions, how can you hold yourself and those beliefs to account? It takes a little soul-searching and self-reflection to consider where changes in thinking may in fact be changes for the better.

As a thoughtful person, you have the strength of character to not only reflect on your moral code, but to also admit when you've been wrong. Your willingness to remain open to change is a willingness to hold your beliefs to account and to live a life of high moral standards.

You adopt a flexible approach: Following on from the above, your openness to change means you're not stuck in your ways. To build good character, you need to know who you are, and you need to know what you value, but to live a morally high life, you also need to remain open to different points of view.

Morality is not clear cut, and while you might expect those with high morals to be very rigid in their ways, this is not the case. Take a moment to think back to the moral dilemmas presented in Chapter 2. Doing the right thing is not always straightforward, and different situations may necessitate a different approach. It takes strength of character to stay true to yourself, but it takes flexibility to do your best and do the right thing when faced with a moral dilemma.

You strive for fairness: In order to be fair, you need to be able to see beyond yourself and to consider the bigger picture. This means being selfless.

With strong moral character, you are able to remain objective, even when emotions are running high. You display good judgement, and you strive to ensure it's always one rule for everyone – no picking and choosing to suit your own purposes. Of course, what's *fair* is subject to different interpretations, but your desire to be fair and just in all you think and do compels you to do the right thing by everyone, leaving no one feeling hard done by.

Double Standards?

When you have strong moral character, you're not easily swayed by popular opinion. You are open to change, and you are flexible, but you are not someone who changes their opinion or stance just to fit in with whoever is around them at the time.

Something that's very interesting is that, according to a study published in the *British Journal of Psychology*, there's a lot more hypocrisy surrounding moral claims than you might think. In fact, the participants in the study who were most harsh in their judgement of others tended not to apply the same judgement to themselves. For example, many of those claiming the moral high ground on behaviours such as lying or cheating often did so to boost their social standing rather than because they truly stood by those values. The claims they made were sometimes based on *saying* the right thing, or what they believed would be considered the right thing, not necessarily what they would *do* themselves. Where they readily pointed the finger of blame at others, they were able to find mitigating circumstances when it came to themselves. In other words, the study highlighted that some people choose to adopt a one-rule-for-me-and-another-for-everyone-else attitude in life.

Of course, the researchers involved in the study made a point of recognising that it was only one study and one small set of findings, but they did conclude that it's perhaps wise to be a little cynical about moral claims. Not everyone who claims to live by the golden rule of treating others as you would wish to be treated yourself is living up to that claim.

Just as not all teenagers are layabouts or troublemakers and not all taxi drivers are jobsworths, not all politicians are liars, and not all social media influencers are frauds. However, sometimes expectations must be defied, and this is where being someone of good character with high moral standards becomes even more important. *Who* you are is not just who you say you are, it's who you show yourself to be in all you think, say, and do. It's who you consistently are, not just who you are from time to time when it suits the mood or circumstances, and it's who you can be relied upon to be. Being someone of good character with high moral standards is being your best self – always.

Successful Character Traits

Now is a good time to take a look at the character traits known to be shared by successful people, and to note how many of them have already been included in the chapters of this book. Success means different things to different people, but those who strive to achieve their goals and become the best they can be in life have the following characteristics in common.

Leadership: Successful people are typically strong leaders. To achieve what you want in life, you need to find your own path, not just follow others. Other people may not want what you want, so only by choosing to lead can you get on track to achieving *your* dreams.

Self-Confidence: To be a success, you must believe in yourself as a success – albeit a success in the making. Having confidence in yourself and your abilities gives you what you need to go after your goals *and* stay on track to achieving them, even when things don't always go to plan.

Aspiration: Great people *aspire* to be great. Knowing exactly what it is you aspire to achieve is a key element of successfully achieving it. Successful people set themselves *specific* goals, not vague targets, and they put smaller step-by-step goals in place to keep them moving towards the big goal.

Drive: Successful people often talk of feeling driven to succeed. They feel passionate about achieving their goals and this provides the motivation needed to keep going after them – and more. It's inner drive that allows dreams to become realities.

Patience: Successful people know that there's no such thing as an overnight success. Success requires effort, and it must be consistent effort – day in and day out.

Someone wise once said that there are no shortcuts to any place worth going, and successful people know this. They know that patience is a virtue, and good things come to those who wait, but they also know that they must keep working hard to keep moving towards those good things coming their way.

A good way to think about this is to imagine setting yourself the goal of running a marathon. If you're new to running, this is not something you're going to be able to do instantly, or without a progressive training plan. In the early stages, it may seem there's little to show for your efforts, but each one of those efforts is an accumulative step towards the desired outcome. The only way to succeed is to keep taking one small step at a time.

Discipline: Alongside the traits of drive and patience, successful people also have discipline. It's self-discipline that allows them to keep working hard and remain consistent in their efforts to achieve, and it's also behind the development of successful habits and routines that keep everything on track.

Communication: Successful people are effective communicators. No one makes it to the top of their game on their own, so those who achieve know the importance of being a team player, and the value of good communication.

Integrity: To truly succeed, success must be yours without compromising your values. Integrity is remaining true to yourself and what matters most, and demonstrating integrity in all you do earns you respect. Authenticity and honesty help to form strong relationships built on trust, and that trust brings the people you need to help you succeed into your life.

Willingness to Learn: Successful people are lifelong learners. They know that no one knows everything, and they know that knowledge is power. They are always open to new ideas and trying different approaches, meaning they are always challenging themselves to be better.

Responsibility: Everyone makes mistakes, but those who succeed in life take full responsibility for their every action – irrespective of whether it leads to success or failure. Only by taking responsibility can lessons be learned from mistakes made, and only by owning up to errors can improvements be made next time.

Self-reliance: Another shared trait of successful people is self-reliance. Teamwork and collaboration are important, but being self-reliant allows you to overcome obstacles and make progress on your own, thereby boosting your learning.

Optimism: Successful people are typically optimists, but they are also realistic. This means they are able to remain positive despite the inevitable setbacks and challenges they face. Being able to visualise a successful outcome is an important element of making it happen.

Passion: It's often said that successful people do what they love and love what they do. The more passionate you are about achieving something, the more motivated you are to do whatever it takes to achieve it. It's always going to be easier to do what you *want* to do, rather than what you feel you *have* to do, or *should* do, and passion makes every part of the journey to success so much more enjoyable.

Creativity: Successful people also tend to be creative. This is not to say that every successful person has creative abilities such as writing or painting, it simply means they have an openness to thinking creatively. They never allow themselves to be constrained by convention, or to become stuck in their ways, and this allows them to experiment with new approaches to solving problems or making improvements. Creative thinkers stand out from the crowd.

Resilience: You already know that success is not an overnight process, and success is rarely the result of one isolated action. It takes repeated action to succeed, so it takes resilience, because not every action you take will bring the desired outcome. Resilience in the face of failures or obstacles allows you to persevere and try again until you succeed. This is one of the most important traits that successful people share because it's a trait that keeps them on track to becoming all they can be. With resilience, there's no giving up on goals.

Chapter 6 Standout Points

❶ The benefit of building good character with high moral standards is that you become someone who has what it takes to *always* remain true to yourself.

❷ Being authentic and staying true to your values is always more important than being "popular" or fitting in.

❸ You earn respect by giving respect.

❹ Everyone matters, but other people's opinions of you don't matter. Who chooses to like or dislike you is not your concern.

❺ *Who* you are is not just who you say you are, it's who you show yourself to be in all you think, say, and do. It's who you consistently are, not just who you are from time to time when it suits the mood or circumstances, and it's who you can be relied upon to be. Being someone of good character with high moral standards is being your best self – always.

Chapter 7

Living a Virtuous Life

In the last chapter, you learned that successful people know *patience is a virtue*, but have you ever stopped to consider the meaning of the word virtue, or what it means to live a virtuous life?

Dictionary definitions of virtue include "behaviour showing high moral standards" or "a quality considered morally good or desirable in a person", so living a virtuous life is choosing to live your life in accordance with these qualities. The virtues you choose to live by can be considered your own moral code, therefore they influence every decision you make in day-to-day life, and being someone of good character is at the heart of making the "right" choice, or doing the right thing. In a nutshell, a good way to think about it is to see living a life of virtue as choosing to love and respect the world around you.

With that said, if you type "list of virtues" into a search engine, you're going to find a mind-boggling number of lists to pick and choose from. Some include hundreds of virtues, others list relatively few, so how do you know which ones are *the* virtues to live by? To answer this question, you need to reflect on everything that makes you stand out from the crowd for the right reasons. In chapter 1, honesty, authenticity, integrity, responsibility, respectfulness, humility, and perseverance are highlighted as positive character traits. These traits can be considered virtues to live by as a morally good person, but as you know, morals are only guidelines. The morals held by one individual can be quite different to those held by another, and they're not fixed.

Morality is a topic that has been mulled over for hundreds of years. Aristotle, the Ancient Greek philosopher, narrowed his thoughts down to a list of 12 virtues that he listed as truths to live by. They are:

Courage – this means living bravely, rather than being defined by your fears.

Temperance – this means living a life of moderation, rather than seeking joy in material wealth.

Liberality – this means living freely without self-imposed restrictions.

Magnificence – this simply means being charismatic and moving through life with style.

Magnanimity – this means maintaining a spirit of generosity.

Ambition – this means taking a healthy sense of pride in all you do.

Patience – this means maintaining a calm approach in life and being good-tempered.

Friendliness – this means being social and open to forming new relationships.

Truthfulness – this means living honestly and with sincerity in all you do.

Wit – this means choosing to see the funny side of life and to maintain a sense of humour.

Modesty – this simply means keeping your ego in check throughout life.

Justice – this means being guided by truth and a moral sense of right and wrong in your every thought and action.

Of course, the world is constantly changing, and morals along with it, but a more recent take on defining moral thinking is provided by modern-day philosopher, Alasdair MacIntyre. He suggests three questions to ask yourself:

Who am I?

Who ought I to become?

How ought I to get there?

Answering these questions will get to the heart of being who you want to be, and then always doing the right thing as that version of you. Moral theologian and author James F Keenan also proposes that thinking morally and living a virtuous life goes beyond thinking of individual characteristics, stating, "Being virtuous is more than having a particular habit of acting, e.g., generosity. Rather, it means having a fundamental set of related virtues that enable a person to live and act morally well".

What Would Superman Do?

A fun way to imagine how you might get yourself out of a tricky situation is to ask yourself, *what would superman do?* This might not always provide a practical solution, but it serves to demonstrate the power of looking to a positive role model for guidance on how to think and act in any given situation. Okay, Superman is a fictitious character, *but*, we all know how he would think and react, and how he would use his superpowers to save the day, right? He's everything we think of in terms of being a good person and doing the right thing, so even though he's not real, we can still aspire to be more like him. It's interesting to note that the word virtue comes from the Latin word *virtus*, meaning power, worth, or force. This means that aspiring to live a virtuous life is a great way to acquire those superpowers after all!

It's fair to say that for many people, the idea of living a virtuous life conjures up images of living a life of no fun at all. It has somehow become associated with being a "goody two-shoes" or being an unrealistic do-gooder prone to interfering in the lives of others. Perhaps there *are* some individuals who consider themselves "holier than thou", and some who look down from their high horses with a sanctimonious attitude, but these people are *not* living a virtuous life. There is no love and respect being shown to the world around you if you are being condescending or smug – no matter how "good" you might consider yourself or your behaviour to be.

In the children's story that popularised the "goody two-shoes" expression, a little girl named Margery

Meanwell is an orphan with only one shoe. After a rich gentleman gives her a new pair, she proceeds to tell everyone about it, going around shouting, 'Two shoes! Two shoes!' to the point of becoming unbearably smug in the eyes of others. The moral of the tale is that good fortune should never become something to gloat about. Think about it: was Superman ever smug about saving the world?

Complementary Virtues

A virtue is a positive character trait, and while we might not believe ourselves to be in possession of every trait included in a lengthy list of virtues, we all have positives in our character. Recognising these positives is simply recognising your strengths. "Play to your strengths" is a common expression, but if all your focus is on utilising something you already have, there's potential for weaknesses to be overlooked rather than improved. If strengths are being used to compensate for weaknesses, there's a danger that you can become a victim of those strengths. For example, if self-discipline is a strong trait in you, the complementary trait of flexibility may be underdeveloped. Or, if compassion and kindness are strengths, self-assertiveness could be a weakness, leading to other people taking advantage of your good nature. The point being made is that playing to strengths is important, but recognising weaknesses and choosing to develop them is equally important if you are to become the best you can be and live a life of fulfilment.

Here's another list of virtues with similar traits grouped together:

- Acceptance. Letting go.
- Contentment. Joyfulness.
- Confidence. Boldness. Courage. Assertiveness.
- Forgiveness. Magnanimity. Clemency.
- Honesty. Authenticity. Truthfulness. Sincerity. Integrity.
- Kindness. Generosity. Compassion. Empathy. Friendliness.
- Loyalty. Trustworthiness. Reliability.
- Perseverance. Determination. Purposefulness. Tenacity.
- Willpower. Self-control. Fortitude. Self-discipline.
- Loyalty. Commitment. Responsibility.
- Caring. Consideration. Support. Service.
- Cooperation. Unity.
- Humility. Simplicity.
- Creativity. Imagination.
- Detachment.
- Wisdom. Thoughtfulness. Insight.
- Dignity. Honour. Respect.
- Energy. Motivation. Zest. Enthusiasm. Passion.
- Resilience. Grit. Tolerance. Patience.
- Excellence.
- Orderliness. Purity. Clarity.
- Prudence. Awareness. Tactfulness. Preparedness.
- Temperance. Balance. Moderation.
- Justice. Fairness.
- Trust. Faith. Hope. Optimism.
- Calmness. Serenity. Centredness. Peace.
- Gratitude.
- Grace. Elegance. Gentleness.
- Flexibility. Adaptability.

Take a moment to ponder over the above virtues and make a note of where you believe your strengths and weaknesses lie. Next, consider if any of your strengths may be traits that you display "to a fault". If you are "caring to a fault", could you be prone to smothering others with kindness at times? If you are "calm to a fault", could you be in danger of lacking enthusiasm and passion? You see, even when it's a positive trait, too much of it isn't always a good thing. There needs to be balance in all things; virtues included.

When balance is achieved, living a virtuous life allows you to...

Live more compassionately.

Be in tune with others.

Live without guilt or shame.

Navigate difficult circumstances.

And make decisions you are proud of.

Finding balance may seem like a tall order, but it's found in simply striving to be your best in all you think, say, and do. Remember, it's not about being *the* best, it's being *your* best – and being someone who stands out for the right reasons.

Putting Virtues into Practice

Let's take a look at what it means to put virtues into practice in daily life.

Honesty

The quality of being fair, truthful, and trustworthy.

Being honest is being truthful in everything you think, say, and do. This is sometimes easier said than done, especially when it means having to admit to making a mistake or being in the wrong. Sadly, being *dis*honest has almost become a way of being in some aspects of life, particularly where being economical with the truth is considered nothing more than "getting ahead" or "getting a foot in the door". Popular TV programmes such as *The Apprentice* demonstrate just how far from the truth certain "ambitious" individuals are prepared to stray in their attempts to get ahead, or get one up on fellow contestants. The problem is, what they perceive to be little lies actually end up having big consequences as they inevitably catch up with them. The more little lies you're prepared to tell, the bigger a liar you become in the eyes and minds of others. You earn a reputation as someone who can't be trusted or taken at their word.

Your moral compass is your guide to what's right and what's wrong, so it's your guide to truth and honesty. The honest option is not always the easy option, and being honest can, at times, place you at a disadvantage, but **honesty really is the best policy**. A story that circulated on social media helps to highlight the benefits of honesty in a real-world situation.

After being pulled over by a police officer for speeding, the driver of the car chose not to look for excuses or argue that they were innocent. Instead, they owned up to having driven faster than the speed limit, even though it hadn't been intentional, and accepted that they should be given a speeding ticket. While the officer was processing the ticket, another driver was pulled over. This driver instantly began to argue with the police officers, stating that they had not been speeding... there were no speed limit signs... the equipment being used must have given a false reading... and the only possible explanation must be a faulty speedometer in the car – which was, of course, not theirs.

A ticket was handed to the original driver as the police officer turned to assist his colleague with the argumentative driver. When the driver looked at it, there was no fine indicated. It read: "Thank you for your honesty. Have a safe drive".

Another story serves to demonstrate that honesty is more than just a one-off action, **it's *who* you are.**

A labourer had been working at a fruit farm for two years. He had shown himself to be a hard-working, trustworthy employee. When the farm manager approached the owner to accuse the labourer of stealing, the farm owner chose to investigate the matter, rather than take the manager's word for it. It transpired that the farm manager was in fact the thief. He was stealing fuel and attempting to cover his tracks by charging it to the worker's vehicle.

The labourer's honest character and good name went before him, and this proved to be of far greater value than the "authority" of the manager when the false accusation was made.

Respect

The quality of treating others with courtesy and consideration.

Respect is living by the Golden Rule of treating others as you would wish to be treated yourself. It means accepting others for who they are, even when they're different to you, or they don't share your opinion.

When you show respect, you bring a sense of trust into your relationships with other people, and being respectful of others earns you respect in return. Simple ways to put respect into practice include:

- Really listening to what others have to say.
- Giving your full attention to those you interact with.
- Acknowledging that other people also want to speak and be heard.
- Putting yourself in the shoes of another so that you can show compassion.
- Recognising differences, but also remaining open to finding common ground.
- And treating other people's property with the same care you would your own; always asking permission before using or taking.

There's a tale about a beggar and a baker that beautifully showcases the quality of **treating others with courtesy and consideration.**

One day, a beggar in extremely shabby clothes entered a popular bakery. All the other customers in the shop looked away with contempt, holding their noses. Nevertheless, the baker behind the counter welcomed the beggar warmly.

The beggar carefully took some coins out of his pocket and whispered to the baker that he wanted to buy a small cake. After picking a small but perfect cake from the shelf, the baker handed it to the beggar, bowing to him as he did so and thanking him for his custom.

After the beggar left, the baker's grandson looked perplexed. He wanted to know why his grandpa had treated the beggar so nicely. To answer this question, the baker said, 'The money he gave me is money he has begged for from others, little by little and one coin at a time, making it even more precious than the money others have. His choice to spend the money here means he must truly love our cakes.'

In response, his grandson then asked, 'So why did you accept his money?'

The baker replied, 'He came to our shop to buy the cake; we must respect him. If we didn't charge for the cake, it would be an insult to him.'

Integrity

The quality of sticking by moral values, even when it's difficult or unpopular.

You already know that having integrity is choosing to do the right thing, even when no one is watching. It's all about doing what's best, rather than what's easy, and doing what's congruent with your values. In everyday life, this means choosing not to distort the truth to suit your own purposes, or think in terms of what you might "get away with" if you keep quiet, and staying true to your word. In other words, you can be relied upon to be you – as your best self.

Life is sometimes likened to a game of golf. Moving around the golf course, playing from one hole to the next, is like moving through life, "playing" each new stage as it comes along. Just as every swing a golfer makes won't lead to a hole in one, the same can be said of life. Not every move you make will bring the desired outcome, but it's not game over; you can play on and take another swing at it. Perhaps the most important thing of all is that golf is a game of integrity, and the game of life should be considered the same.

In golf, players score themselves, so they also call penalties on themselves whenever a rule is broken. One very important rule is that a golfer must play the ball "where it lies", meaning that if the ball lands on rough ground, for example, the player can't pick up the ball and move it to smoother ground – even if it's just a short distance away – before playing their next shot. If they do, it should be marked on their scorecard as a shot taken. PGA Associate Jacob Williams explains integrity on the golf course by saying, "The idea behind moral integrity in golf is simple: do what you believe is right regardless of how it might affect your score or playing status. It means more than just abiding by the rules; it also involves fair play, respect for others, honesty about one's performance, acceptance of responsibility for mistakes or bad shots, and self-discipline in order to act responsibly even when no one else is watching. It also requires avoiding any form of cheating or taking advantage of other players' mistakes through intentional manipulation or distraction. Moral integrity in golf means doing what is morally right even when it may not always be comfortable or convenient".

However, not all golfers abide by the rules, and not all display the traits of moral integrity. As in golf, so it is in life! Getting away with something because no one is looking may seem like a good way to get ahead, but the more it's done, the more it becomes your reputation. If you claim to play shots that others consider to have been impossible, your integrity becomes questionable. No one wants to play a round of golf with a cheater, and no one wants to spend time in life with someone who can't be relied upon to play fair.

An online story from *Golf Upgrades* about a golfer named Eddie helps to highlight the benefits of **playing golf and life with integrity**.

Eddie was an up-and-coming professional golf player whom everyone knew to have a strong sense of moral integrity. He would always play fair, be kind to his opponents, and never take shortcuts that might give him an edge. One day, as he came close to sinking the winning putt for the tournament, Eddie realised he had forgotten to count the penalty strokes, accidentally giving himself the competitive advantage. After much internal deliberation, Eddie stepped back from the ball and took the penalty strokes – forfeiting any chance at winning the game. But in doing so, he earned eternal respect from fellow golfers by exemplifying true moral integrity on and off the course.

"Moral integrity is like a sturdy tree planted with deep roots of solid values and beliefs. When faced with challenges, the branches may sway and bend, but they will never break" – *Golf Upgrades*.

Compassion

The quality of showing empathy and kindness towards those who are suffering or in need.

Compassion is being able to put yourself in another's shoes and feel what they're feeling as if it's happening to you. This puts you in a better position to offer help, or to do something to alleviate suffering. Showing compassion is caring about another person and building true human connections. In everyday life, compassion can be shown in so many simple ways: offering a word of encouragement or advice; listening without judgment; helping someone in need, directly or indirectly; volunteering; teaching; assuming the best in others; and doing something for someone who can never repay you.

Something it's important to note is that compassion and sympathy are not one and the same. As one wise, anonymous author once wrote:

"Sympathy looks in and says, 'I'm sorry.' Compassion goes in and says, 'I'm with you.'

Sympathy looks in and says, 'I would like to help.' Compassion goes in and says, 'I am here to help.'

Sympathy says, 'I wish I could carry your burden.' Compassion says, 'Cast your burden on me.'"

Let's say you notice someone struggling to carry a bundle of items along a busy street, eventually dropping them all over the pavement. With sympathy, you're going to feel sorry for them and wish you had time to help – but you're running late and need to get to work. With compassion, you're going to notice the struggle and step in to ask if you can help. Compassion is opening your heart to others, and doing what you can for others. Even the smallest of compassionate acts can make a big difference in another person's life.

Mother Teresa is a name synonymous with compassion. She dedicated her life to assisting the poor and destitute in India and beyond. She once said...

"If you are kind, people may accuse you of selfish, ulterior motives: be kind anyway. If you are successful, you will win some false friends and true enemies: succeed anyway. If you are honest and frank, people will try to cheat you: be honest anyway. What you spend years building, someone could destroy overnight: build anyway. If you find serenity and happiness, they may be jealous of you: be happy anyway. The good you do today will often be forgotten by tomorrow: do good anyway. Give the world the best you have, and it may never be enough: give your best anyway".

Generosity

The quality of sharing with others, whether it's skills, money, time, attention, or any other resource, with no expectation of anything in return.

A generous person is a giving person, but true generosity is found in the person who gives for no other reason than because they can. Being generous to be recognised as a generous person, or to be applauded for an act of generosity, is not demonstrating the true spirit of generosity. You might remember that the virtue of generosity is grouped together with the virtues of kindness, compassion, empathy, and friendliness, and there's an old folktale from India that serves to highlight the power of giving.

Paying it Forward

A poor woman had only one son. She worked hard cleaning houses and grinding grain for the well-to-do families in town. They gave her some grain in return and she lived on it. But she could never afford to buy nice clothes or toys for her son. Once, when she was going to market with some grain to sell, she asked her son, 'What can I bring you from the market?'

He promptly replied, 'A drum, Mother, get me a drum.'

The mother knew she would never have enough money to buy a drum for her son. She went to the market, sold the grain, and brought some gram flour and some salt. She felt sad that she was coming home empty-handed, so when she saw a nice piece of wood on the road, she picked it up and brought it home to her son.

The son wasn't sure what to do with the stick, but he smiled and carried it with him when he went out to play. He came upon an old woman lighting her woodstove with some cow-dung patties. The fire was not catching and there was smoke all around making the old woman's eyes water. The boy stopped and asked why she was crying. She said that she couldn't light her fire to cook. The boy said, 'I have a nice piece of wood that you can have to start your fire with.' The old woman was very pleased. She lit the fire, made some bread, and gave a piece to the boy.

Taking the bread with him, he walked on until he came upon a potter's wife. Her child was crying. The boy stopped and asked her why the child was crying. She said the child was hungry and she had nothing in the house to give him. The boy gave the bread he had in his hand to the hungry child, who ate it eagerly and stopped crying. The potter's wife was grateful to the boy and gave him a pot.

When he walked on, he came to the river, where he saw a washerman and his wife quarrelling. The boy stopped and asked the man why he was scolding his wife. The washerman said, 'This woman broke the only pot we had. Now I've nothing to boil my clothes in before I wash them.' The boy handed over the pot he had been given and asked that they stop quarrelling. The washerman was very happy to get a large pot. He gave the boy a coat in return.

Walking on, the boy came to a bridge where he saw a man shivering in the cold without so much as a shirt on him. He asked the man what had happened to his shirt, and the man said, 'I was coming to the city on this horse. Robbers attacked me and took everything, even my shirt.'

The boy said, 'Don't worry. You can have this coat.' The man took the coat, and to thank the boy for his kindness, he asked that he should take his horse.

The boy took the horse. Soon, he ran into a wedding party, but the bridegroom, his family, and the musicians were all sitting under a tree with long faces. The boy stopped and asked why they looked so glum. The bridegroom's father said, 'We're all set to go in a wedding procession. But we need a horse for the bridegroom. The man who was supposed to bring it hasn't arrived. The bridegroom can't arrive on foot. It's getting late, and we'll miss the auspicious hour for the wedding.' So, the boy offered them his horse, and they were delighted.

When the bridegroom asked him what he could do in return, the boy said, 'You can give me something: that drum your musician is carrying.' The bridegroom had no trouble persuading the drummer to give the drum to the boy, who now rushed home to his mother, beating his new drum, eager to tell her how he came to have it… beginning with the nice piece of wood from the roadside.

The moral of the tale is that giving should always be without expectation of anything in return, and we should pay kindness and generosity forward by being kind to someone else after kindness is shown to ourselves.

To put the spirit of generosity into a modern-day context, a real-world story conveyed by Siobhan Kukolic, a life coach in Canada, provides a perfect example. She writes:

> "A teacher friend of mine was teaching math to a class of six-year-olds, a number of whom were recently-arrived refugees from other countries. The topic was fractions. My friend defined what a half and a quarter were, and then asked the children to write down whether they would prefer a half or a quarter of a chocolate bar. As she walked around the room, she noticed that some of the new students wrote they would prefer a quarter of the chocolate bar. My friend thought she would have to re-teach the lesson, as they didn't appear to understand that a half was bigger than a quarter. She asked the students why they would prefer a quarter of the chocolate bar and one little girl replied, 'So that more people could have a piece of chocolate.' I cried when I heard that story. It reminded me how beautiful humanity is if we take a moment to notice it".

It can seem that we live in a world where generosity is often forgotten, but there is a quote from Seneca that indicates it's perhaps a virtue we have always needed to be reminded of:

> "We should give as we would receive, cheerfully, quickly, and without hesitation; for there is no grace in a gift that sticks to the fingers".

Humility

The quality of believing yourself to be no better than anyone else; recognising that no one is perfect, and admitting to mistakes and shortcomings.

In everyday life, humility is shown in being humble. With humility, your thoughts and actions are not driven by vanity, arrogance, or inflated feelings of self-importance. It's *not* all about you. You have no need to compare yourself against others, and you are able to feel genuinely happy for others when they succeed. Ralph Waldo Emerson perhaps said it best when he said, "A great man is always willing to be little". Humility is letting go of any desire to feel superior to other people, either by means of wealth, fame, intelligence, beauty, titles, or influence. You don't consider yourself to be any more or any less than anyone else, or as C S Lewis put it, "True humility is not about thinking less of yourself; it is thinking of yourself less".

In everyday life, humility is being able to apologise when you're wrong; accepting that losing is simply part of learning, and that you don't always need to win to succeed; leading by example, not considering yourself too superior to get your hands dirty; being open to accepting feedback and constructive criticism; recognising your limitations, and not being embarrassed to ask for help; understanding that everyone has something to learn, and that everyone can be your teacher; and being respectful of different points of view.

In short, practicing humility is *not* allowing your ego to rule your life, and it's the moral taught in the Aesop's fable, *The Wolf and the Lion*.

Roaming by the mountainside at sundown, a wolf saw his own shadow become greatly extended and magnified.

He said to himself, *Why should I, being of such an immense size and extending nearly an acre in length, be afraid of the lion? Ought I not to be acknowledged as king of all the collected beasts?*

While he was indulging in these thoughts, a lion fell upon him and killed him. He exclaimed with a too late repentance, 'Worthless me! This overestimation of myself is the cause of my destruction.'

Gratitude

The quality of being thankful for what you have in life and taking the time to appreciate it.

According to Roman philosopher Cicero, gratitude is not only the greatest of the virtues, but the parent of all the others. In a nutshell, gratitude is experiencing a sense of happiness and thankfulness for everything positive in your life. "Gratitude is an attitude" is a common expression, and it sums up the benefits of choosing to see the bigger picture, even on days when things don't appear to be going your way. It's all too easy to get so caught up in what's going wrong that you fail to notice everything that's going right. Practicing gratitude in everyday life is as simple as taking the time to notice and appreciate all the good things you already have.

"Gratitude is a powerful process for shifting your energy and bringing more of what you want into your life. Be grateful for what you already have, and you will attract more good things" – Rhonda Byrne.

Useful ways to develop an attitude of gratitude include:

Keeping a Gratitude Journal

At the end of each day, jotting down three good things that happened to you, or things to be grateful for, is a good way to turn your focus to the positives in your life. After all, it's quite possible that you experience many happy moments in any given day, only to forget about them by the next day as your focus returns to negatives.

Expressing Your Gratitude

How often do you take the time to tell the people who matter most to you in life just how much they mean to you? If you feel gratitude, share it.

Celebrating the Small Things

It's fair to say that we're conditioned to celebrate big achievements in life, perhaps overlooking all the smaller achievements in day-to-day life. Taking the time to acknowledge "little wins" as they happen is a great way to remind yourself of the good things you have to be grateful for.

Perseverance

The quality of sticking with it and keeping on going despite obstacles or setbacks.

As you already know, success is rarely the result of a one-off action, it takes repeated positive actions. Whatever it is you want to achieve in life, you need to be prepared to stick with it for as long as it takes to get there. Successful people develop successful habits, and establishing a habit takes perseverance.

Let's say you want to get fit; it's not something you're going to achieve after one session at the gym. Let's say you want to lose weight; it's not something you're going to achieve after saying no to one chocolate bar. Let's say you want to get a promotion; it's not something you're going to achieve after proving yourself to be a candidate on one occasion. To achieve any of these things, you need to *keep* doing what needs to be done, until what you want becomes what you are – you can only become better through perseverance.

Everyone knows The Beatles. They are one of the most famous bands in the history of music, but they didn't set out to be famous, they set out to make a great record. When they achieved a great record, they set about achieving another great record. The goal wasn't to be the best, it was simply to make the best record they possibly could. One great record at a time, the band became a global phenomenon. What this teaches us is that perseverance is not just something that's needed for a far-off goal, it's needed in everyday life. It's a virtue that allows you to be your best in *everything* you do, and always doing your best keeps you on track to becoming the best you can be.

Forgiveness

The quality of letting go of anger, resentment, or bitterness, making it possible to move on.

It's a sad fact that people will let you down in life. Social media is full of stories of disappointment, heartache, broken promises, and betrayal. These things are likely to happen, but they don't need to define your life – unless you choose to let them.

Holding on to feelings of anger or hurt is like holding on to a heavy weight that you continue to carry around with you wherever you go. The heavier the weight, the more it's going to drag you down and hold you back. Forgiveness is the process of letting go, and thereby freeing yourself from the heavy burden. Of course, when you've been hurt by someone, this is easier said than done, and this is why forgiveness is a virtue.

To put forgiveness into practice, the most important thing to realise is that forgiveness isn't something you do for the other person. To forgive, you don't need to excuse the other person's actions, and you don't even need to tell them they're forgiven. Forgiveness is *not* forgetting the upset ever happened, and choosing to forgive does *not* mean you need to let the other person back into your life. Forgiveness is something you do for *you*, and you do it so that you can move on in life. Author Joan Lunden perhaps said it best when she said, "Holding on to anger, resentment, and hurt only gives you tense muscles, a headache, and a sore jaw from clenching your teeth. Forgiveness gives you back the laughter and the lightness in your life".

Clearly, putting any of the above, or any other virtue into practice is an ongoing process. As good character traits, virtues are not just what you do, they are who you are, and who you are is shown in every little thing you think, say, and do every day. Living a virtuous life is living life as the person you aspire to be – but remembering that no one is perfect.

Chapter 7 Standout Points

❶ Living a life of virtue is choosing to love and respect the world around you.

❷ A virtue is a positive character trait, and we all have positives in our character. Recognising these positives is simply recognising your strengths.

❸ The word virtue comes from the Latin word *virtus*, meaning power, worth, or force. This means that aspiring to live a virtuous life is a great way to acquire superpowers!

❹ Too much of a good thing isn't always a good thing. There needs to be balance in all things; virtues included.

❺ Living a virtuous life is living as the person you aspire to be – but remembering that no one is perfect.

Chapter 8

The Shortness of Life

Have you ever not done something because "life is too short"? If you've used those words, it was probably because the something you chose not to do was something you considered to be boring, or just too much effort, right? Most of us consider life to be too short to waste time on dull tasks, but in this chapter, it's time to consider how much of our lives we still waste on things that really don't matter at all.

In the grand scheme of things, life *is* short, but this doesn't mean your life can't be a life well lived. As we're often reminded, no one on their death bed ever regrets not spending more time at the office. The message here is that a life well lived is a fulfilling life, leaving no room for regrets. So, what is a fulfilling life, and how do we go about living it? Well, it's all about living a life of meaning.

Finding Meaning

Finding meaning in your life is finding your own "why'" in life. Your why is found in understanding what you value, and what matters most to you. For this reason, everyone's "why" is going to be different. Fulfilment comes from finding a deep sense of satisfaction in what you do, so it's found in devoting your time and energy to the things that matter most. Of course, there are always going to be aspects of life that don't fill you with a sense of satisfaction – that's life – but with the right attitude, the best can be found in every moment.

Living a fulfilling life isn't necessarily about changing your circumstances, it's much more to do with your attitude to your circumstances. When you are able to go through each day with a sense of remaining true to yourself, even the most difficult of times can feel easier to manage. Your circumstances don't define you.

"Circumstances do not make the man, but reveal him" – James Allen.

You already know that staying true to yourself can be challenging in a world that creates pressures from every angle. There's pressure to look a certain way; pressure to be popular; pressure to be (or at least appear to be) successful; pressure to conform, pressure to achieve, accomplish, and get ahead; and perhaps even pressure to earn a certain income… the pressures of modern life, and very often the pressures of others' expectations, can make it difficult to just be yourself, and to stay true to who you want to be. If you're not being true to yourself, are you living the life you want to live, or could you be in danger of putting your own hopes and dreams on hold for another day – only to find that you have run out of days?

Finding Fulfilment

Taking the time to discover what gives you a sense of meaning and purpose in your life is going to help you find greater fulfilment in all you do.

Check in with yourself

Life can become so busy that it's easy to lose sight of what really matters most to you. Checking in with yourself is taking the time to reflect on how you are spending your days, and then holding what you find up against what is important to you. Have you got your priorities right? Or have you allowed other pressures to push what really matters to the bottom of your to-do list? Getting back on track to living a life of fulfilment begins with making *your* priorities an actual priority!

However, there will always be tasks that need to be done, and there will often be things that are more urgent than the things you want to do, so checking in with yourself is not about beating yourself up over choosing to put those priorities at the top of your list. Simply taking the time to recognise that there's a mismatch between the way your time is being spent and the way you would like to be spending it is an important step towards looking for opportunities to fit more of the things that represent fulfilment into your life.

In a series of blog posts, Arianna Huffington asked her followers to tell their stories of "wake-up calls" that led to changes for the better in life. One follower told the story of putting her all into climbing the career ladder. For years, she put her work before everything else, pursuing what she believed to be success. However, the realisation that her all-work-no-play life might be something she'd come to regret compelled her to make a change. She resigned: "What ensued was a year and a half journey that took me through Brazil, the Middle East, and India. Eventually it brought me back to what I was looking for all along; myself. I realised that I had been silencing my passions, instead of nurturing them."

Make small changes

Depending on your circumstances, checking in with yourself might lead you to question whether there's *anything* fulfilling in the life you're currently living. If this is the case, change is clearly needed, but finding fulfilment doesn't need to involve drastic action. It's well documented that radical changes are unlikely to be lasting changes, and that step-by-step changes are much more likely to be maintained. For example, rather than suddenly quitting your career and embarking on humanitarian work, look for ways to bring more of what matters most to you into your daily life. With the right attitude, there are opportunities all around you to do more of what matters and to be who you want to be. Are there any community projects you could get involved in? Do you have skills or knowledge you could share with others to help them achieve their goals? Do you have spare time that could be put to good use in a volunteer role? Perhaps a change of career is ultimately the right move for you, but taking small steps in the direction you would like to go is a great way to begin making the things that matter most to you much more of a priority in your daily life. Each day of greater fulfilment grows into weeks, months, years... and a life of fulfilment.

"One step at a time you can change your life, one step at a time you can go from average to great, don't be disheartened on the journey to a greater life. Everyday do something in relation to your goals, have a daily task list of things that need to be completed and get them done, if you don't get them complete on that day take it over to the next day, but make sure you make positive strides towards the life of your dreams" – Asad Meah.

Be Grateful

It's important to note that if you've reached the point of believing there's *nothing* fulfilling in your daily life, you may have allowed negative thinking to cloud your view. Stopping to "smell the roses" and to be grateful that those "roses" are there can help open your eyes, mind, and heart to all the good things you already have in life. Recognising those good things and appreciating how good they make you feel can be a positive reminder of what *really* matters. Could it be that you've simply stopped noticing the things that bring you joy? To live a life that's fulfilling, you need to make space to see and feel everything that's positive. If negative thinking is clouding your view, your focus will only ever be on what's missing, and what's *not* bringing you joy.

"Stop to smell the roses" is an expression used as a reminder to slow down at times in life, and to take a moment to appreciate the simple pleasures of everyday life. As many wise people have said, "enjoy the little things, for one day you may look back and realise they were the big things".

A great example of this is found in Thornton Wilder's stage play, *Our Town*. Set in the early 20th century, the story deals with the preciousness of life – and time. After the main character, Emily, dies in childbirth, she asks to be able to return to Earth to look upon one day in her life. She chooses her 12th birthday. She watches the day's happenings in the kitchen, living room, and outside the house, but notices that even though her family are with one another, no one seems to notice anyone else. They go about their busy lives, preoccupied. Eventually, she cries out, even though no one can hear her, 'Oh, Mama, Mama, just look at me, look at me for a minute, as though you really see me, just for a moment now, while we're all together. Mama, let's be happy. Let's look at one another and really see each other.' But, their lives just go on. Realising this, Emily turns to the stage manager character and says, 'Life goes so fast. We don't even have time to look at one another. I didn't realise this while I was living. We never noticed.' Saddened, almost broken-hearted, she asks to leave the day behind. As she's leaving, she looks back over her shoulder and says, 'Goodbye world; goodbye Grover's Corners; goodbye Mama and Papa; goodbye taste of coffee; goodbye new-ironed dresses; goodbye clocks ticking, and hot baths; goodbye sleeping and waking. Oh life, oh life, you're too wonderful. Why don't we realise?'

Live in the moment

Following on from the above, living in the here and now is an important element of appreciating all you have. For example, if your thoughts are constantly focused on how much better your life will be when you achieve some future milestone or goal, you are likely to be living your life with a distinct sense of being *un*fulfilled. It's good to have goals, but if the journey towards achieving them isn't enjoyable, you're in danger of wishing your life away. There are no guarantees in life, so making the most of each moment and each day is an essential step in building a life of fulfilment.

"It is not in the pursuit of happiness that we find fulfilment, it is in the happiness of pursuit" – Denis Waitley.

How many things have you put off doing because you were waiting for the time to be right, or waiting for all your ducks to be in a row in some other way? How many times have you told yourself that once you achieve x, y, or z, then you'll be happy? If you keep telling yourself that having that one thing will make your life perfect, you're going to find that there's always another "one thing" coming along that you need to make your life perfect... Aspiring to achieve and be more is good, but putting off happiness until you get there is not.

To live a fulfilled life, you need to find a way to be happy with life *now*. One way to do this is to pay attention to the simple pleasures in everyday life, and another is to celebrate every little win each day. Instead of waiting to cross whatever self-imposed finish line you've created for yourself before celebrating, choose to celebrate every little step you take towards that finish line. After all, there's no defined finish line in life! As the saying goes, "don't put off until tomorrow what can be done today". This doesn't just apply to chores that need done, it also applies to finding joy in what you already have. Happiness isn't something to put on hold for another day, it's something you can find all around you *every* day if you look for it.

If you're always waiting for "that day" when everything will change for the better, you're missing out on everything that's good in your life *today*. There's a real danger of becoming *someone* who is never quite happy, no matter what they have or what is happening. You become that person who is never quite happy with their job; their home; their appearance; their partner; their friends; their holiday plans... you name it, there's always something you wish was different. When this happens, even changing jobs or moving house can't bring happiness because you're still looking for something better, or you find yourself missing certain elements of what you had. In short, you're never content with what you have.

"Big Yellow Taxi" is a famous Joni Mitchell song. She sings, "Don't it always seem to go that you don't know what you've got till it's gone". The message in the lyrics is a message for life – choose to appreciate all you *have* from one day to the next, rather than having to lose something before fully appreciating what you *had*.

Expect Less?

Expecting less, or lowering your expectations, doesn't mean giving up on big goals or lowering your standards in terms of becoming the best you can be, it means accepting that best doesn't need to be perfect. Unrealistic goals of perfection in every aspect of your life will only lead to disappointment, and each disappointment will add to an overall sense of living an unfulfilled life. No one is perfect; life isn't perfect. Beating yourself up over every error or setback is counterproductive. If you have impossibly high expectations, life can end up becoming a series of disappointments, and instead of enjoying what *is* happening, you find yourself focusing on what you wish was happening instead. Perfectionism can lead to all-or-nothing thinking, and this gets in the way of appreciating what's already good. Choose to accept that things don't need to be perfect, and you open your mind to all the good things that *are* happening right now. Opportunities to feel more fulfilled are everywhere if you allow yourself to see them.

"Can't see the wood (forest) for the trees" is an idiom that fits well with this point. If you get too caught up in details, or you fixate on one small thing, you can become blinkered to the bigger picture. Chasing perfection can get in the way of enjoying all the wonderfully imperfect moments that add up to a happy life.

Build fulfilling relationships

Surrounding yourself with uplifting people is a positive way to feel fulfilled in life. Spending your time with people who inspire and support you in all you do will not only create a feelgood factor in the moment, but it will also help to create a life of happy memories. Building positive relationships with others is an important element of building positivity and a sense of life-well-lived fulfilment into your life. Why waste time with people who only drag you down?

Many of us feel a sense of guilt in putting our own needs ahead of the needs of others, but it's important to look after yourself just as you would choose to look after others. In effect, you need to build a good relationship with yourself before you can build good relationships with others. To give others your best, you need to be your best, and this means taking care of yourself. If you're trying to be all things to all people, or simply a people-pleaser, it becomes impossible to be true to yourself, or to live your life according to your true values.

Yoga teacher Gregory Angell asks his students to think of life as a train journey. He writes:

Life is like a journey on a train, with all its stations, route changes, and delays! At birth, we boarded the train and met our parents, and we believe that they will always travel with us. However, at some station, our parents will step down from the train, leaving us on this journey alone.

As time goes by, other people will board the train. They will be significant, perhaps our siblings, friends, children, and even the love of our life. Many will step down and leave a permanent vacuum. Others will go so unnoticed that we may not even realise they've left their seat. The train ride will be full of joy, sorrow, expectation, hellos, goodbyes, and farewells. Success on this journey revolves around having good relationships with all these passengers, and this means we must give the best of ourselves.

The mystery for all of us is that we don't know at which station we ourselves will step down. So, we must make the most of the journey, living a life of love, forgiveness, and offering the best of who we are. It is important to do this because when the time comes for us to step down and leave our seat empty, we should leave behind beautiful memories for those who will continue to travel on the train of life without us.

Life Is Long Enough

According to the works of Seneca, life is only too short if we waste the time we have. Spending time with negative people who hold you back in life is wasting time. Spending time bouncing from disappointment to disappointment in search of unrealistic perfection is wasting time. Living only for some future dream is wasting the time you have in the here and now, as is failing to notice and appreciate the good things you already have in life. And, always putting everyone else's priorities ahead of your own, or pursuing the dreams others have for you instead of your own is wasting the time you have. He writes:

> It is not that we have a short space of time, but that we waste much of it. Life is long enough, and it has been given in sufficiently generous measure to allow the accomplishment of the very greatest things if the whole of it is well invested. But when it is squandered in luxury and carelessness, when it is devoted to no good end, forced at last by the ultimate necessity we perceive that it has passed away before we were aware that it was passing.

So it is – the life we receive is not short, but we make it so, nor do we have any lack of it, but are wasteful of it.

Everyone hurries his life on and suffers from a yearning for the future and a weariness of the present. But he who bestows all of his time on his own needs, who plans out every day as if it were his last, neither longs for nor fears the morrow. Life is divided into three periods—that which has been, that which is, that which will be. Of these the present time is short, the future is doubtful, the past is certain. Has some time passed by? This he embraces by recollection. Is time present? This he uses. Is it still to come? This he anticipates. He makes his lifelong by combining all times into one.

A Life of Leisure?

Several of Aesop's fables have been included in the pages of this book. Born around 620 BCE, Aesop was a Greek storyteller famed for his stories that taught valuable truths in simple to understand ways. It's believed by historians that many of the fables were written by countless others over the centuries, but Aesop's fame has led to all of them being attributed to him – although some historians question whether he was ever a real person at all!

Living a fulfilling life is all about finding balance. All work and no play is likely to lead to regrets, but the same can be said of a life that's all play and no work! Aesop told this truth in a fable called *The Ant and the Grasshopper.*

On a cold frosty day, an ant was dragging out some of the corn that he had laid up in summertime, to dry it.

A grasshopper, half-perished with hunger, besought the ant to give him a morsel of it to preserve his life.

'What were you doing,' said the ant, 'this last summer?'

'Oh,' said the grasshopper, 'I was not idle. I kept singing all the summer long.'

The ant, laughing and shutting up his granary, said, 'Since you could sing all summer, you may dance all winter.'

Winter finds out what summer lays by.

The moral of the tale is that it takes a little planning ahead to make the best use of time, or, in other words, we should make hay while the sun shines. Of course, if this lesson is taken to extremes, there's a danger of slipping into only ever living for tomorrow and failing to appreciate and enjoy today. In finding balance, you live a life of meaning and purpose with a plan for the future *and* you enjoy the simple pleasures of every day and every step you take towards that future.

"Where your talents and the needs of the world cross, therein lies your vocation. These two, your talents and the needs of the world, are the great wake up calls to your true vocation in life... to ignore this is, in some sense, to lose your soul" – Aristotle.

Chapter 8 Standout Points

❶ In the grand scheme of things, life is short, but this doesn't mean your life can't be a life well lived.

❷ A life well lived is a fulfilling life, leaving no room for regrets. It's all about living a life of meaning.

❸ Finding meaning in your life is finding your own "why" in life. Your why is found in understanding what you value, and what matters most to you.

❹ If you're not being true to yourself, are you living the life you want to live, or could you be in danger of putting your own hopes and dreams on hold for another day – only to find that you have run out of days?

❺ There are no guarantees in life, so making the most of each moment and each day is an essential step in building a life of fulfilment. Life is a balancing act. To find fulfilment, you must balance meaning, purpose, and a plan for the future alongside enjoyment of the simple pleasures that are already yours as you journey towards that future.

Chapter 9

You've Got to Have Faith

In the Beginning

It would seem fair to say that we're living in a world undergoing a substantial shift in its ethical bearings. Today's world has veered away from the doctrines once firmly anchored in religious teachings, and research points to a notable downturn in the number of churchgoers or those with any religious affiliations. Alongside this downturn, there appears to be a marked increase in depression and mental health complications, and this, coupled with the prevailing attitude of instant gratification has developed what feels like an overall slump in moral standards – and these standards are sadly accepted as the "new normal". It's normal (if not encouraged) to put yourself and your own needs ahead of others and their needs, and it's normal for differences of opinion to become shouting-match battlegrounds with neither side able to respect the other's point of view. What happened to empathy, compassion, respect, and even the common decency to listen to others, let alone openly and fairly discuss differences of opinion?

Could there be a correlation between the decline in church attendance and the escalating trend of moral decline? It's a question that's certainly worth pondering over. Individuals seeking wisdom and truth can identify that the current state of affairs is a direct result of the challenge Satan posed to God, as portrayed in the story of Adam and Eve's descent into sin and their subsequent belief that they could not only survive but flourish without adhering to God's laws.

Satan's brazen challenge to God's sovereignty is alarmingly apparent in his cunning suggestion that humanity would do better making their own moral judgments. This allegation was a direct attack on God's sovereignty, questioning His supreme authority and right to guide His creation.

Observing the state of our world, communities, and even our own families, it's clear that people are increasingly distancing themselves from God's moral compass, opting for self-defined ethics instead. However, the disturbing trends across various social metrics highlight our inability to flourish without God's guidance.

As those who continue to uphold God's standards, we must persist in seeking wisdom and understanding, as advised in Proverbs 4:7. We need to be steadfast in cultivating good character and high moral values, boldly standing for what is right over what is popular. We need to stand out, but for all the right reasons. We should consider it a privilege to face ridicule for upholding God's laws. This chapter is intended for those who resist conforming to society's deteriorating norms.

The fact that you've engaged with this text to this point distinguishes you as a seeker of wisdom and understanding, or at least someone curious and open-minded enough to learn more.

Faith and Faithfulness

We're living in an age where moral compromise is increasingly commonplace, making the virtues of faith and character much needed pillars of integrity to help guide believers through life's often choppy waters. Christian faith extends beyond a simple belief; it is an active reliance on God's promises, a light that shines the way to righteousness. This moral compass, with faith as its magnetic north, provides direction in the stormy seas of life. This section aims to delve into the Christian ethos of faithfulness, exploring its significance, necessity, and how it intertwines with good character.

Faith, in Christianity, is the confident conviction of things we hope for and the assurance about what we do not see (Hebrews 11:1). It's more than just acknowledging God's existence, it involves a deep trust in His benevolence, His promises, and His providence. This trust forms the foundation of our relationship with God, and without it, it is impossible to please Him (Hebrews 11:6).

Faithfulness, one of the fruits of the Spirit (Galatians 5:22), encapsulates the consistent commitment to an assignment despite obstacles or delays, therefore it embodies reliability, dependability, and trustworthiness. To the believer, faithfulness is not merely a quality, but a lifestyle; a commitment to God's word and His commandments.

The Bible offers compelling narratives that underscore the importance of faithfulness. Abraham, commonly referred to as the father of faith, is a prime example. Despite numerous challenges, and even in his old age, Abraham remained faithful to God's promise of making him a father of many nations (Genesis 17:5). His faith was not passive, it was active, demonstrated through obedience and trust in God's word.

Similarly, Daniel's story showcases extraordinary faithfulness. Despite a decree outlawing prayer, Daniel remained committed to his prayer life (Daniel 6). His unwavering faith and steadfastness in maintaining his relationship with God provide practical examples of living a life of faith, emphasising the importance of obedience, prayer, and trust in God.

Emulating faithfulness requires a conscious decision to abide by God's commandments and to trust Him fully. This can be achieved by cultivating a personal relationship with God, observing and reflecting on biblical examples of faithfulness, practicing obedience to God's commandments, and trusting in God's promises, even when circumstances seem bleak.

Faith and faithfulness are integral components of Christian character. They serve as guiding lights in a morally compromised world, providing us with a framework for living lives pleasing to God. By understanding and emulating biblical examples of faithfulness, we can navigate life's complexities with integrity and steadfast trust in God's promises, *and* in so doing, we can stand out from the crowd for all the right reasons.

The Signs of the End Times

The signs of the end times, as prophesied in the Bible, guide believers in understanding the final phase preceding Jesus Christ's return and the final judgement. These prophecies, spread across various books of the Bible, provide a sequence of events leading to the ultimate culmination of human history.

The book of Daniel from the Old Testament and the book of Revelation from the New Testament are primary sources detailing end-time events. Key events prophesied include the rise of the Antichrist (2 Thessalonians 2:3-4), the Great Tribulation (Matthew 24:21), the Second Coming of Christ (Revelation 19:11-16), and the Final Judgement (Revelation 20:11-15).

In today's society, several signs align with biblical predictions. The moral decline is evident in the normalisation of sin, as forewarned in 2 Timothy 3:1-5. False prophets and teachers, warned against in Matthew 24:24, abound, distorting biblical truths for personal gain.

An increase in the number of natural disasters such as earthquakes, hurricanes, and wildfires echo Matthew 24:7's prophecy of "earthquakes in various places". Wars and rumours of wars, as mentioned in the same verse, remain prevalent, visible in ongoing conflicts worldwide.

Though the "indicators of the end times" have persisted for thousands of years, it's undeniable that the events described in Matthew are statistically escalating. These signs might be unsettling, yet Christians are encouraged to remain steadfast in their faith, drawing fortitude from the scriptures. Ephesians 6:10-18 implores followers to don the complete armour of God to endure challenging times.

Practical steps towards donning this armour include consistent prayer, meditating on God's word, and fellowship with other believers (Hebrews 10:25). In these ways, Christians can keep their spiritual focus, resisting the allure of worldly distractions. Moreover, Christians should exhibit love and kindness, emulating Christ in their interactions (John 13:34-35). This approach counters the moral decay experienced in society, and presents a beacon of hope to those lost in darkness.

The end times, while daunting, should not incite fear among Christians. Rather, they should serve as a reminder of our eternal home, encouraging us to live righteously. By understanding biblical prophecies, recognising their manifestations, and responding with steadfast faith, Christians can navigate these challenging times with grace and fortitude, eagerly awaiting the return of our Savior.

Embodying the Divine Design: a Roadmap to Flourishing

Our loving Creator designed us with a unique purpose – to lead lives that are fruitful, healthy, and prosperous. This divine design is not simply an abstract concept, but a profound truth deeply embedded within the biblical narrative. From the Genesis account of creation, where God blessed humanity and said, "be fruitful and multiply" (Genesis 1:28), to the New Testament teachings that encourage us to "live a life worthy of the Lord and please him in every way: bearing fruit in every good work" (Colossians 1:10), the Bible consistently echoes this divine roadmap for human flourishing.

The Bible serves as our instruction manual. It can be thought of in the same way as a TV manual being essential for getting the most out of the device as it offers wisdom, direction, and principles to help us navigate the complexities of life.

In today's world, the idea of living up to God's standards might seem abstract or even intimidating. However, when we explore biblical teachings, we realise these standards are practical and relevant, and they can significantly enhance our lives. Values such as forgiveness, integrity, and humility, which are fundamental to Christianity, are not merely spiritual ideals but practical tools for thriving in our day-to-day lives.

Imagine a situation where you have been wronged by someone. Maintaining resentment and anger can be mentally and emotionally exhausting. However, the Bible instructs us to forgive, and when we do, we are freed from the toxic grip of bitterness, leaving us free to find emotional healing and peace. Similarly, integrity allows us to build trust and respect in our relationships, contributing to relational well-being, and humility helps us acknowledge that we don't have all the answers, nurturing a learning attitude and promoting intellectual growth. These examples serve to demonstrate that obedience to God's commands is far from restrictive, it is, in fact, liberating.

Following God's commands leads to thriving in all aspects of life. However, flourishing according to God's standards isn't merely about individual prosperity. It's about reflecting God's love and goodness to the world, influencing others positively, and contributing to societal well-being. For instance, when we practice generosity, another biblical principle, we not only experience the joy of giving, but also do our part in terms of addressing challenges such as poverty and inequality in society.

Ultimately, adhering to God's high standards takes us towards the abundant life that Jesus promised (John 10:10). This abundance isn't limited to material prosperity, but encompasses a fulfilling life – physically, mentally, emotionally, and spiritually. It's about experiencing peace amidst chaos, joy in sorrow, hope in despair, and love in a world filled with hatred.

God's high standards are not burdensome obligations but divine guidelines for human flourishing. As we strive to meet these standards, we discover the joy of living in harmony with God and experience the abundant life He intended for us.

Faith as an Anchor in Troubled Waters

In the Christian faith, the notion of "increased strength" is closely linked to deepening faith in God. As a believer's faith intensifies, so does their spiritual strength, enabling them to face and overcome adversities.

The Bible frequently underlines the connection between faith and strength. In Isaiah 40:31, it states, "but those who hope in the Lord will renew their strength. They will soar on wings like eagles; they will run and not grow weary; they will walk and not be faint". This verse suggests that faith in God grants believers a renewed sense of strength, enabling them to surmount challenges in ways that would otherwise be impossible.

Belief in God endows individuals with a spiritual resilience that transcends human abilities. It provides hope in times of desolation, solace during pain, and certainty amidst ambiguity. Unlike the broader world's experience of such adversities, your experience, fortified by faith, will distinctly set you apart.

Numerous biblical examples illustrate individuals drawing strength from their faith during challenging times. David's victory over Goliath (1 Samuel 17) despite his intimidating size and strength, was not due to David's physical prowess, but his unwavering faith in God. Likewise, Apostle Paul, who faced numerous trials throughout his ministry, remained steadfast in his faith, affirming in Philippians 4:13, "I can do all things through Christ who strengthens me".

The Crucial Role of Faith in Difficult Times

Maintaining robust faith during challenging times is essential for several reasons. Firstly, it provides a source of comfort and hope, reminding believers that God is always with them. Secondly, it strengthens their overall relationship with God. As James 1:2-4 states, "consider it pure joy, my brothers, and sisters, whenever you face trials of many kinds, because you know that the testing of your faith produces perseverance. Let perseverance finish its work so that you may be mature and complete, not lacking anything".

In essence, difficult times can act as a catalyst for spiritual growth, deepening our trust in God and strengthening our faith.

Practical Tips for Reinforcing Faith

Reinforcing faith requires intentional and consistent effort. Here are a few practical tips:

Prayer: Regular communication with God is vital. Pray for strength, wisdom, and guidance. Prayers need not be formal or elaborate. God values sincerity over eloquence.

Reading and Meditating on the Word: Spend time reading the Bible and reflecting on its teachings. This can provide comfort, guidance, and encouragement.

Fellowship: Surround yourself with others who share your faith. They can provide support, encouragement, and accountability.

Faith plays a pivotal role in facing and overcoming adversity. It provides a source of strength, comfort, and hope, enabling believers to endure and overcome difficult times. By maintaining and strengthening your faith, you can deepen your relationship with God, growing spiritually mature and resilient in the face of life's challenges.

Navigating Life's Challenges with God's Peace and Comfort

In the face of life's relentless pressures, it's easy to succumb to stress and anxiety. Yet, as followers of Christ, we have access to a peace that surpasses all understanding, and a comfort that can soothe our weary souls. This divine tranquillity anchors us, even when life's tumultuous waves threaten to capsize us. A peace that is not felt by the world at large.

Philippians 4:6-7 offers a profound reminder of this truth: "Do not be anxious about anything, but in every situation, by prayer and petition, with thanksgiving, present your requests to God. And the peace of God, which transcends all understanding, will guard your hearts and your minds in Christ Jesus." This passage reassures us that when we entrust our worries to God, He rewards us with a peace that defies human logic.

This divine tranquillity during times of stress is something I have personally experienced. When I received a Type 1 Diabetes diagnosis at the mature age of 40 – and shockingly on my wedding day – I could, understandably, have succumbed to feelings of overwhelm, anxiety, and even anger. The reality of having to administer insulin injections four times daily for the rest of my life was daunting. However, when I decided to rely on God, sharing my fears and worries with Him through prayer, I experienced a peace that was unmistakably divine. This realisation highlighted the preciousness of life and empowered me to live a more fulfilled and focused existence. Consequently, it made me stand out from the crowd in all the best ways.

Scripture is replete with individuals who sought and found God's peace during their trials. David, despite being relentlessly pursued by King Saul, consistently sought God's strength and peace. In Psalm 62:5-6, David declares, "yes, my soul, find rest in God; my hope comes from him. Truly he is my rock and my salvation; he is my fortress; I will not be shaken".

Relying on God's strength extends beyond finding peace and comfort when facing stormy seas in life, it also offers wisdom, providing a means of navigating through life's uncertainties. Proverbs 3:5-6 advises, "trust in the Lord with all your heart and lean not on your own understanding; in all your ways submit to him, and he will make your paths straight". This scripture suggests that trusting God's wisdom over our limited human understanding results in wise decisions and clear paths. This is a stark contrast to the prevailing worldly approach of setting personal standards and rules for living.

The Transformative Power of Forgiveness

Forgiveness is a cornerstone of Christianity, emphasised by Jesus Christ as crucial to maintaining harmonious relationships. In Matthew 18:21-22, He teaches that forgiveness should be limitless, a continual attitude rather than an occasional act.

Faith in God empowers Christians to forgive others, even when it seems insurmountable. Corrie Ten Boom, a Holocaust survivor, was able to forgive her brutal captors because of her faith in God. Her story exemplifies how faith can facilitate the release of resentment and anger, leading to healing and improved relationships. Once again, this contrasts sharply with today's prevailing don't-get-mad-get-even mindset.

Kindness: A Reflection of God's Love

Kindness is another Christian principle that significantly influences relationships. Ephesians 4:32 states, "be kind and compassionate to one another, forgiving each other, just as in Christ God forgave you". When we exhibit kindness, we mirror God's love for us, transforming our interactions with others.

Mother Teresa dedicated her life to showing kindness to the impoverished and sick in Calcutta, India. Her faith in God fuelled her compassion and selflessness, inspiring millions worldwide. Her actions demonstrate how kindness, rooted in faith, can foster empathy and understanding, promoting healthier relationships.

By trusting in God, individuals can improve their relationships through the practice of forgiveness and kindness. These principles, deeply embedded in Christian teachings, foster reconciliation, empathy, and love – all vital for healthy relationships.

To implement these principles, you can begin by reflecting on your relationships and identifying areas requiring forgiveness, or more kindness. Regular prayer can also be beneficial, offering a platform to seek God's guidance and strength. Lastly, acts of service can help actualise kindness, allowing individuals to experience the joy and fulfilment that comes from selflessly serving others. Needless to say, this is yet again a sharp contrast to the self-centred what's-in-it-for-me attitude that's painfully common in today's world.

By embracing forgiveness and kindness, individuals can not only strengthen their relationship with God, but also enhance their relationships with others, creating a ripple effect of love and harmony.

Steering Through Life's Ups and Downs

Life is a blend of highs and lows, triumphs and defeats, joys, and sorrows. During challenging times, it's easy to lose sight of our path and feel overwhelmed. However, these trials and tribulations are the very moments when our faith is put to the test and fortified. James 1:2-4 encourages us to "consider it pure joy, my brothers and sisters, whenever you face trials of many kinds, because you know that the testing of your faith produces perseverance".

Living a life grounded in the principles of the Bible provides us with heightened clarity and focus. It enables us to trust in God's plan, navigate life's trials and tribulations, and move confidently towards realising our dreams. As Christians, we must continually strive to deepen our faith and let it guide our actions and decisions. Only then can we experience the peace and fulfilment that stems from living a life aligned with God's purpose for us.

"Trust in the Lord with all your heart and lean not on your own understanding; in all your ways submit to him, and he will make your paths straight" – Proverbs 3:5-6.

Experiencing the Joy of Gratitude

As we nurture an inner sense of gratitude, we begin to encounter a profound joy that is independent of our circumstances and deeply rooted in our connection with God. This joy is distinct from the fleeting happiness offered by worldly pleasures. It is a deep-seated, enduring joy that emanates from knowing and trusting God. Scripture tells us that the joy of the Lord is our strength (Nehemiah 8:10).

This divine joy equips us to confront life's challenges with bravery and a positive outlook. It infuses our lives with hope and positivity, enabling us to appreciate life's beauty in all situations. By rekindling our faith, we foster gratitude, leading to a life filled with joy. Even when events don't unfold as planned, or hopes aren't immediately fulfilled, we can choose to remain thankful and joyful, knowing that God is in control and orchestrating everything for our good (Romans 8:28).

The Advantages of Upholding High Moral Standards

In an era where moral relativism often reigns supreme, the advantages of adhering to high moral standards, especially those set forth in God's Word, remain a timeless testament to the transformative power of godly living. These standards serve as a guiding compass, steering us through life's complex labyrinth, providing protection against the perils associated with low moral standards, and unlocking the abundant blessings that stem from obedience to God's commands. Here are some examples.

The Priceless Benefits of Sexual Purity

Not just a safeguard against sexually transmitted diseases or unintended pregnancies, sexual purity is a commitment to honouring God with our bodies, acknowledging the sanctity of our sexuality, and preserving our physical and emotional well-being. When we live in alignment with God's commands regarding sexual purity, we establish a strong foundation for healthy, rewarding relationships.

We foster self-discipline, respect for others, and a deeper appreciation of the beauty of love within marriage. The life of Joseph, as recounted in Genesis 39, provides a compelling testament to the rewards of maintaining sexual purity. Despite intense temptation from Potiphar's wife, Joseph chose to honour God rather than yielding to fleeting pleasure. His commitment to purity not only saved him from a potentially disastrous situation, but also set the stage for greater blessings and advancement in his life.

The Deep Blessings of a Godly Marriage

God's standards provide an impeccable blueprint for a successful and fulfilling marriage. When couples commit to each other for life, promising to remain together "till death do us part", they create a stable environment conducive to nurturing love, trust, and mutual respect. A godly marriage, as outlined in the Bible, is characterised by sacrificial love, mutual submission, and unyielding commitment.

It is a union that encourages personal growth, nurtures emotional intimacy, and offers an ideal setting for raising godly children. The story of Ruth and Boaz in the Book of Ruth beautifully illustrates the blessings of a godly marriage. Their mutual respect, selfless love, and steadfast commitment to each other and to God resulted in a lasting relationship that brought joy, satisfaction, and divine favour. Their legacy extended beyond their lifetime, with them becoming ancestors to King David and, ultimately, Jesus Christ.

What a contrast this is to contemporary views on matrimony! We live in a world where divorce is readily sought the moment a relationship becomes "difficult". A world where individuals desire a church wedding, despite having no connection to the institution, and no intention of ever returning. A world where reality TV glamorises the idea of "marriage at first sight". A world where vows are exchanged in front of an Elvis impersonator while other love-struck (yet very often soon to be divorced) couples impatiently wait their turn. This is far removed from God's original design for marriage. Given these circumstances, it's hardly surprising that 42% of marriages in the UK end in failure, leading to emotional distress, financial strain, and single-parent households.

The Wide-ranging Benefits of Honesty and Trustworthiness

Honesty and trustworthiness form the cornerstone of a life lived according to God's standards. The commandments against lying and stealing (Exodus 20:15-16) are not mere prohibitions, they are invitations to live a life marked by peace, integrity, and robust relationships. When we choose honesty over deceit, we foster trust in our relationships, promote fairness, and maintain a clear conscience before God and people. We also contribute to building a just society where truth is valued and upheld.

The biblical accounts of King David and Daniel provide contrasting lessons on the outcomes of honesty and dishonesty. David's dishonesty, leading to Uriah's death, resulted in family discord, public disgrace, and divine displeasure (2 Samuel 11-12). In contrast, Daniel's unwavering honesty and integrity, even when faced with potential death, led to his promotion, preservation, and favour with both God and men (Daniel 6). Adhering to high moral standards as set by God is not merely beneficial – it's transformative. It positively impacts our physical health, emotional well-being, relationships, and inner peace.

As Christians, our commitment to these standards should not stem from a sense of obligation or fear of punishment, but from a deep love for God and an understanding of the abundant life He desires for us. To live by high moral standards is, in essence, choosing to live life to its fullest extent.

Chapter 9 Standout Points

❶ Today's world has veered away from the doctrines once firmly anchored in religious teachings, and research points to a notable downturn in the number of churchgoers or those with any religious affiliations. Could there be a correlation between the decline in church attendance and the escalating trend of moral decline?

❷ Observing the state of our world, communities, and even our own families, it's clear that people are increasingly distancing themselves from God's moral compass, opting for self-defined ethics instead.

❸ We need to be steadfast in cultivating good character and high moral values, boldly standing for what is right over what is popular. Christian faith extends beyond a simple belief; it is an active reliance on God's promises, a light that shines the way to righteousness. This moral compass, with faith as its magnetic north, provides direction in the stormy seas of life.

❹ Faith, in Christianity, is the confident conviction of things we hope for and the assurance about what we do not see (Hebrews 11:1). It's more than just acknowledging God's existence, it involves a deep trust in His benevolence, His promises, and His providence.

❺ In an era where moral relativism often reigns supreme, the advantages of adhering to high moral standards, especially those set forth in God's Word, remain a timeless testament to the transformative power of godly living. These standards serve as a guiding compass, steering us through life's complex labyrinth, providing protection against the perils associated with low moral standards, and unlocking the abundant blessings that stem from obedience to God's commands.

Chapter 10

Standing Out in Summary

Standing out in life is being the best version of you it's possible to be. Here are the standout points from each chapter, and some further tales and words of wisdom to reflect on.

Chapter 1 – Standing Out for the Right Reasons

Standing out for the right reasons is all about who you are and how you present yourself in what you do.

It's true that we should never judge a book by its cover, but it's also true that first impressions matter. In all aspects of life, the way you present yourself and the way you behave become the impression you make on others.

Establishing a good name for yourself is a key element of standing out for the right reasons; your name is the reputation that goes before you.

The impression you make on others then becomes associated with your name. The amazing thing about a "good name" or a "bad name" is that the impression you make on one person can become your reputation – and your reputation may go before you, even among people who have never met you in person.

If you want to have a good reputation, you need to earn it. It's not about striving for perfection; it's simply striving to be the best you can be.

A good name is not something you can buy, and keeping a good name requires consistency in everything you do. It takes time to establish a reputation, but all it takes to destroy a good reputation is one ill-judged moment. What you *say* is of no value if it's not what you *do*. Saying you're a hard worker means nothing if you don't back up your words with actions. Saying you're a loyal friend means nothing if you fail to demonstrate it when it matters most in your friendships. It's what you do that becomes your reputation. If you often say one thing but then do another, all you establish is a reputation for being someone who can't be trusted or relied upon.

To be able to live a fulfilled and contented life, you need to find your own path to being all you can be.

Making a good name for yourself is part and parcel of making a mark for yourself in life. Whatever it is you want to achieve in life, or in your career, there's no space for sitting back and resting on your laurels. To make a mark, you must always give your best, and if you always put a best effort into all you do, your best will keep on getting better. Just like establishing a good reputation, making a mark for yourself in life is standing out for the right reasons. For example, in a job interview, what will make you stand out from all the other candidates with the same list of qualifications on paper? In a workplace environment, what will make you stand out from your work colleagues when the opportunity to go for promotion arises? In both scenarios, the answer is your character. It's not about being better than anyone else, it's about being your best self.

Good character makes you stand out, and you can work on developing stand out character traits by being positive, being engaging, and being a good communicator.

Your character is who you are *and* what you consistently do. To be consistent, you need to be genuine, not fake. Being authentic is being "the real thing". Individuals with good character always stick by what they believe in, and stand up for what they believe to be right, they don't change their stance to curry favour with others. Being positive, engaging, and a good communicator allows you to express who you are and what you value, and then matching your actions to your words demonstrates your sincerity in everything you say and do. Developing good character is ensuring you always show yourself in your best light and your true colours always shine through.

Your True Colours

An interesting approach to interviewing candidates for a job vacancy demonstrates how someone's behaviour can influence the interviewer's opinion of their character. The company boss in question used an all-day interview process with multiple candidates. This meant lunch was included. Any candidates who put salt, pepper, sauce, or any other condiment on their food before tasting it would go no further in the interview process. Irrespective of CVs or qualifications, the outcome of his "salt and pepper test" ruled his decisions. Why? Because he believed this behaviour revealed something about an individual's true character – they were unwilling to try something before judging it. Food for thought, isn't it?

Chapter 2 – The Importance of Morals and Values

Morals are the guidelines we live by. They help us to develop a strong sense of right and wrong, and to make good choices in life.

Morals teach us how to behave in a socially acceptable way, how to treat other people around us, and to understand the consequences of our actions. They are therefore something we acquire through experience and from the example shown to us by the people who care for us when we're growing up. We then gain further experience from the wider community as we get older and interact with different people.

An individual's morals may be influenced by cultural or religious beliefs, and those beliefs can vary hugely around the globe.

Morals aren't necessarily fixed; they can shift and change. The morals you live by govern the way you behave and the choices you make in life. The things you value and the principles you stand by in life help to influence your every decision, motivating you to do the right thing. If we think of morals as right or proper behaviour, then values are what we believe to be right or wrong behaviour. In other words, we learn morals through society or religion, but values come from within.

There isn't always a clear "right" or "wrong" response in every situation, it comes down to *your* character and *your* values.

In everyday life, it's often the small dilemmas we face and the on-the-spot decisions we make that shine a light on our true moral character. For example, a package is delivered to your home that should have gone to a different address. The label on it indicates it's an item you want for yourself, but can't afford to buy. Do you keep it, or do you notify the delivery company/ take it to the intended address? The tale of Robin Hood is another great example. Is stealing from the rich to give to the poor morally right or wrong?

Your character is only ever as strong as your core values and beliefs.

Your character can be defined as the qualities or behaviours that identify you as an individual, but *your* character is only ever as strong as *your* core values and beliefs. The way you think and behave is always your choice, so this means your character is your choice. Becoming someone of strong moral character isn't something that happens by accident, it's something you need to intentionally do.

Having a sense of morality is choosing to do the right thing for the right reasons; it's choosing to treat other people fairly and with kindness, or to simply treat others as you'd wish to be treated yourself.

While it's true that an individual's morality may be guided by cultural traditions, each one of us is ultimately responsible for our own moral standards and values. Morals may vary from person to person, mainly through the influences of upbringing and cultural norms, but everyone has some sense of morality. Being true to yourself and what you believe to be morally right is the only route to making *your* world a better place.

Feelgood Stories of Strong Moral Character

These stories reported in newspapers demonstrate that there are good people in the world who choose to do something for other people for no reason other than it being "the right thing" to do.

Lillian Weber was a 100-year-old who sewed a dress a day for children in need. She believed that everyone should have something pretty to wear, and her goal was to sew 1000 dresses by the time she turned 100. On the day of her birthday, she had sewn 1051 dresses for the Little Dresses for Africa charity. The charity founder and director, Rachel O'Neill, said, "Lives are really saved because of these dresses. When a little girl is wearing a new dress, they're much less likely to be messed with because someone knows they're being taken care of".

Willie Baronet, an artist from Texas, travels around the US buying carboard signs from homeless people he meets along the way. The sale can be of vital importance to the homeless person, but Willie makes the purchases in the hope of being able to raise awareness of homelessness through his art.

Cesar Larios found himself stuck in an elevator with an elderly woman. Facing a lengthy wait for rescue, he turned himself into a "human bench" to allow the woman to sit down.

"You left your window open, so I put a bag over it to keep your interior dry. Have a great day!". A note with this message was found by the car owner on their return. This act of kindness saved the car from getting soaked in a rainstorm.

Chapter 3 – The Decline of Moral Values and Its Impact on Society

Cultural norms have changed. Respect for elders and those in authority has changed. News stories of police officers, nurses, and teachers having to deal with abusive behaviour are common, and in many areas, where once there was neighbourliness, politeness, and general kindness towards others in the local community, there is now hostility, rudeness, and no community spirit whatsoever. The question is, does it need to be this way?

Numerous studies suggest that many people believe moral values to be in decline. They believe this because they see a change in the way people behave and interact with one another, and a general shift in attitude away from helping one another to looking out only for themselves. For some, basic kindness appears to be in decline, and anyone might be forgiven for seeing today's world as a place where looking out for number one has become the norm, and trampling over other people to get ahead is simply part of the process.

"It's not whether you win or lose, it's how you play the game". Standing out in life should be standing out for the right reasons.

"Doing well for yourself" appears to have become more important than *how* you do it. Getting to the top of the career ladder at all or any cost appears to be an attitude that young people are encouraged to adopt. Workplaces have become competition fields with everyone claiming to be a "team player" yet always looking out for themselves. Winning is the goal, but the competitiveness of the "me-first" attitude or selfishness of the "what's in it for me?" attitude has perhaps spilled over into all areas of life, leading to a lack of consideration or concern for other people. What's more important to you; being *the* best, or being *your* best? In the game of life, is it more important to win, or to play well?

Becoming someone of strong moral character isn't something that happens by accident, it's something you need to intentionally do.

Your character is shown in who you are and in what you do – consistently. It's in your every thought, word, and action. An accidental kindness or a one-off kind gesture doesn't make you kind!

The values you live your life by are *your* choice. Showing kindness to others is your choice; treating yourself and others with respect is your choice; caring for other people, and protecting the vulnerable is your choice, and so is *not* doing any of these things.

Trying to reduce our carbon footprint is something we're much more conscious of in today's world. The more you can do to reduce it, the more you're doing to help save the planet. How about doing all you can to improve your emotional footprint? This means doing all you can to improve the way you treat other people and to reduce the potential for your words and actions to have a negative impact on them. Standing by good moral values creates a positive emotional footprint that can only serve to improve the quality of your life and the lives of everyone around you.

Good morals are infectious. If you smile at someone, they'll often smile back at you in return. If you treat someone with kindness, they will often return that kindness, or extend it to someone else.

It can be argued that society today is, on the whole, less kind than in previous generations. It can be argued that the increasing busyness of modern life is to blame, and it can be argued that the way we respond to other people, especially strangers, has changed because we fear getting involved in someone else's business or we fear causing offense. However, "doing the right thing" can create a ripple effect – like dropping a pebble into still water – and the "right thing" becomes the norm for everyone touched by the expanding ripple.

Pay it Forward

"When someone does you a big favour, don't pay it back… pay it forward" is the tagline for the 2000 film, *Pay It Forward*. The plot revolves around Trevor, a seventh-grade student in Las Vegas. After his social studies teacher assigns the class to put into action a plan that will change the world for the better, Trevor devises a "pay it forward" plan. This means anyone who has a favour done for them must then do a favour for three other people in return. The only stipulation is that these favours must be something the recipient can't do for themselves.

Back in 2014, a real-life pay it forward movement made the headlines. A woman in Florida started it in a Starbucks drive-thru when she paid for her own coffee and also asked to pay for a caramel macchiato for the driver behind her... who then chose to do the same for the next customer. After people ordered their drinks and drove up to the window, barista Vu Nguyen explained that the drink had already been paid for and asked if they'd like to return the favour. In total, 378 people agreed to keep it going. The baristas thought that if the chain lasted until closing, they would put the remaining money on a gift card and continue the next day, but the chain ended when the 379th customer declined to pay it forward.

The kindness shown by the 378 pay it forward customers is admirable, but it can be argued that it's not in the true spirit of Trevor's plan because those 378 people were in a position to be able to pay for their own coffee. However, the story inspired many other pay it forward schemes, one of which was in Wartman's pizza restaurant in Philadelphia. Mason Wartman explained that a customer could donate an extra dollar when they paid for their pizza. This donation was then indicated on a Post-it note stuck on the wall. A homeless person could then come into the shop and cash in the Post-it note for a free slice of pizza. At the time of explaining the scheme in 2015, over 10,000 slices of pizza had been given away.

However, paying it forward doesn't need to involve actually paying for something, it's all about doing something for someone else. After reading the book by Catherine Ryan Hyde that inspired the film of the same name, Sarah-Jayne Wright realised that the world really would be a better place if everyone just did three favours for others. Having lost her own father at the age of eight, she had great empathy for the children of a family friend who had just been widowed. She took time out to chat to the children, helping to ease their fears and lighten the burden on their mother in such difficult times. This prompted her second "favour" which was to set up a counselling service at her school, particularly to help children dealing with bullying. Her third favour was for her neighbour, an elderly woman who was losing her sight. As this neighbour had been an avid reader, and the one to introduce Sarah Jayne to the *Pay it Forward* book, it was a very real and fitting act of paying it forward for her to take time out every night to read aloud to her, and provide a little company.

Chapter 4 – How to Restore Morality in Society

You are not responsible for the way everyone on Earth chooses to think and behave, you're only responsible for your own thoughts and actions... "You must be the change you wish to see in the world".

During the 1960s and 70s, Arleen Lorrance was a high school teacher in Brooklyn. She was becoming increasingly aware of the violence and poverty her students were experiencing in their lives and decided to try to improve the situation through improving their education. She encouraged them to believe a better life was possible, and by practicing what she preached, she *showed* them how to make change happen for themselves. In effect, she created the change she wanted to see in the world by *being* that change in all she thought, said, and did. In her words, "you must be the change you wish to see in the world".

Each and every one of us *can* help to make the world a better place. Change *can* happen when each of us takes personal responsibility for the way we think and act.

We're only responsible for our own thoughts and actions, but if we all do what we believe to be the right thing to do, the collective effort *will* make a difference.

There will always be individuals with a selfish doesn't-apply-to-me attitude, but that doesn't mean there's no point in choosing to live your life by your own moral standards.

In other words, if everyone else is doing it, does that make it okay for you to do it? If everyone else appears to be throwing litter on the ground, does that make it okay for you to do the same? If everyone else is parking on double yellow lines, does that make it okay for you to do the same? The answers you give to these questions reveal a great deal about *your* moral standards. Standing out is choosing not to follow the crowd when they're heading in a direction that takes you away from all you value.

You can't change the world on your own, but you can change your corner of it, and the ripple effect will expand your reach.

Complaining about the actions of other people won't change anything if you're doing exactly the same. To stand out, you need to think and act differently, and in so doing, demonstrate that there is a better way. If you always strive to be your best and do your best, you become a positive influence on others.

The key to making the world a better place is to keep striving to be better ourselves.

Leo Tolstoy once said "everyone thinks of changing the world, but no one thinks of changing himself". Change needs to come from each one of us as individuals first. If each one of us begins each new day with thoughts of being better than we were yesterday, we can positively influence the world around us, adding value to the lives of everyone in our communities.

Make a Difference

There's a popular story about a lady and some turtles that teaches the importance of always choosing to do what you can to make a difference in the world.

There was once a man who walked his dog every Sunday morning around a lake near his house. Week after week, he saw the same elderly woman sitting at the edge of the water with a small metal cage next to her.

The man's curiosity finally got the better of him and he approached the woman one day. He noticed that the cage was actually a small trap and she had three small turtles in it. In her lap, there was a fourth turtle that she was carefully wiping down with a sponge.

The man greeted her and said, 'May I ask, what do you do with these turtles every week?'

She smiled and explained to him that she was cleaning their shells because any algae or scum that builds up on a turtle's shell reduces its ability to absorb heat and slows down their swimming. It can also corrode their shell and weaken it over time.

The man was impressed as the woman continued, 'I do this every Sunday morning to help the turtles.'

'But don't most turtles live their entire lives with algae on their shells?' the man asked. The woman agreed that was true. He replied, 'Well then, you're kind to do this, but are you really making a difference if most turtles don't have people around to clean their shells?'

The woman laughed as she looked down at the small turtle on her lap. 'Young man, if this little turtle could talk, he would say I'm making all the difference in the world.'

The moral of this story can be summed up perfectly by some wise words from Dr Suess: "To the world you may be one person; but to one person you may be the world".

The message is that you may not be able to do *everything* or help *everyone*, but this is no reason to do *nothing*. Always do what you can.

Chapter 5 – How to Build Good Character with High Moral Standards

Having good character and high moral standards means doing the right thing, and the right thing isn't always the easy option.

To be true to yourself, you need to know who you are and what matters most to you. Armed with this knowledge, you can make choices that fit with being your best self.

The *right* choice for you is the one that aligns with the best version of you. The more you push yourself, the more you grow.

Let's say you find yourself with a choice of project to take on in your workplace. One of them would take only a matter of hours to complete because you've done plenty of others just like it, but the other one involves new instructions and a different approach. Clearly, the first option represents the easy option, but the second option represents an opportunity to grow your skills and expand your thinking.

Surround yourself with people who already demonstrate the qualities you aspire to have. Whatever it is you respect and admire in others can become something others recognise in you when you choose to immerse

yourself in an environment that encourages you to be and do better.

If you spend time with positive people, their positivity rubs off on you. If you spend time with people who always choose the opportunity to grow over the easy option, their disciplined attitude rubs off on you. If you spend time with people you admire for any reason, the qualities that make them admirable in your eyes rub off on you.

To be the best you can be, use each new day as an opportunity to be just that little bit better than the previous day. It's not about being "the best" or being the winner, it's simply being all you can be – one step and one day at a time.

Building good character takes consistency and authenticity in your every thought and action, and it requires a commitment to being and doing your best. Whatever it is you want to change or improve, begin by creating a clear picture in your mind of what it looks like when you've achieved it. Next, make a plan that takes you from where you are to where you want to be, and then take one step at a time to get there.

The Miller, His Son, and Their Ass is an Aesop's fable that teaches the importance of knowing who you are and what matters most to you. To build good character, that character must be built around *your* core beliefs and values.

A miller and his son were taking their ass to a market to sell him. They had not gone far when they met with a troop of girls returning from the town, talking and laughing. 'Look there!' cried one of them, 'did you ever see such fools, to be trudging along the road on foot, when they might be riding!'

The old man, hearing this, quietly bade his son get on the ass, and walked along merrily by the side of him. Presently, they came up to a group of old men in earnest debate. 'There!' said one of them, 'it proves what I was saying. What respect is shown to old age in these days? Do you see that idle young rogue riding, while his old father has to walk? Get down, you scapegrace! And let the old man rest his weary limbs.'

Upon this the father made his son dismount and got up himself. In this manner they had not proceeded far when they met a company of women and children. 'Why, you lazy old fellow!' cried several tongues at once. 'How can you ride upon the beast, while that poor little lad there can hardly keep pace by the side of you?'

The good-natured miller stood corrected and immediately took up his son behind him. They had now almost reached the town. 'Pray, honest friend,' said a townsman, 'is that ass your own?'

'Yes,' said the miller.

'Oh! One would not have thought so,' said the townsman, 'by the way you load him. Why, you two fellows are better able to carry the poor beast than he you!'

'Anything to please you,' said the old man; 'we can but try.'

So, alighting with his son, they tied the ass' legs together and by the help of a pole endeavoured to carry him on their shoulders over a bridge that led to the town. This was so entertaining a sight that the people ran out in crowds to laugh at it, till the ass, not liking the noise or his situation, kicked asunder the cords that bound him and, tumbling off the pole, fell into the river.

Upon this the old man, vexed and ashamed, made his way home, convinced that by endeavouring to please everybody he had pleased nobody, and lost his ass in the bargain.

Chapter 6 – Benefits of Building Good Character with High Moral Standards

The benefit of building good character with high moral standards is that you become someone who has what it takes to *always* remain true to yourself.

Actress Judy Garland once said, "always be a first-rate version of yourself; not a second-rate version of someone else". It's perhaps human nature to compare ourselves to others, but there's nothing to be gained from trying to achieve an unrealistic goal that's based on something entirely fake.

Being authentic and staying true to your values is always more important than being "popular" or fitting in.

When you have integrity, no matter what the latest trends, you will never compromise who you are and what you value. This is not to say you're unwilling to compromise on other things, you're just not prepared to be anything other than your authentic self – even if it means not "fitting in" at times. You stick by your values and you follow your own path.

You earn respect by giving respect.

In your eyes, we are all equal in this world. You treat everyone you meet with the same level of respect, irrespective of differences in culture or opinion, and you remain open to different points of view.

Everyone matters, but other people's opinions of you don't matter. Who chooses to like or dislike you is not your concern.

You don't need to be validated by others to feel good about who you are, and you know that by being true to yourself, the people you need to help you become the best you can be will be attracted into your life.

Who you are is not just who you say you are, it's who you show yourself to be in all you think, say, and do. It's who you consistently are, not just who you are from time to time when it suits the mood or circumstances, and it's who you can be relied upon to be. Being someone of good character with high moral standards is being your best self – always.

Is there anything original, unique, or even authentic in anything you do if you're just trying to be all things to all people?

There's another Aesop's fable that teaches the perils of trying to be all things to all people. It's called *The Man and His Two Wives*.

In days when a man was allowed more wives than one, a middle-aged bachelor, who could be called neither young nor old, and whose hair was only just beginning to turn grey, must needs fall in love with two women at once and marry them both. The one was young and blooming and wished her husband to appear as youthful as herself. The other was somewhat more advanced in age and was as anxious that her husband should appear a suitable match for her.

So, while the young one seized every opportunity of pulling out the good man's grey hairs, the old one was as industrious in plucking out every black hair she could find. For a time, the man was highly gratified by their attention and devotion, till he found one morning that, between the one and the other, he had not a hair left.

He that submits his principles to the influence and caprices of opposite parties will end in having no principles at all.

Chapter 7 – Living a Virtuous Life

Living a life of virtue is choosing to love and respect the world around you.

Dictionary definitions of virtue include "behaviour showing high moral standards" or "a quality considered morally good or desirable in a person", so living a virtuous life is choosing to live your life in accordance with these qualities. The virtues you choose to live by can be considered your own moral code, therefore they influence every decision you make in day-to-day life, and being someone of good character is at the heart of making the "right" choice, or doing the right thing.

A virtue is a positive character trait, and we all have positives in our character. Recognising these positives is simply recognising your strengths.

Moral theologian and author James F Keenan proposes that thinking morally and living a virtuous life goes beyond thinking of individual characteristics, stating, "being virtuous is more than having a particular habit of acting, e.g., generosity. Rather, it means having a fundamental set of related virtues that enable a person to live and act morally well".

The word virtue comes from the Latin word *virtus*, meaning power, worth, or force. This means that aspiring to live a virtuous life is a great way to acquire superpowers!

A fun way to imagine how you might get yourself out of a tricky situation is to ask yourself, *what would superman do?* This might not always provide a practical solution, but it serves to demonstrate the power of looking to a positive role model for guidance on how to think and act in any given situation. Superman is everything we think of in terms of being a good person and doing the right thing, so even though he's not real, we can still aspire to be more like him!

Too much of a good thing isn't always a good thing. There needs to be balance in all things; virtues included.

If you are "caring to a fault", could you be prone to smothering others with kindness at times? If you are "calm to a fault", could you be in danger of lacking enthusiasm and passion? Playing to your strengths is important, but recognising weaknesses and choosing to develop them is equally important if you are to become the best you can be and live a life of fulfilment.

Living a virtuous life is living as the person you aspire to be – but remembering that no one is perfect.

Finding balance may seem like a tall order, but it's found in simply striving to be your best in all you think, say, and do. Remember, it's not about being *the* best, it's being *your* best – and being someone who stands out for the right reasons.

"Virtue lies in our power, and similarly so does vice; because where it is in our power to act, it is also in our power not to act" – Aristotle.

Chapter 8 – The Shortness of Life

In the grand scheme of things, life is short, but this doesn't mean your life can't be a life well lived.

Have you ever not done something because "life is too short"? If you've used those words, it was probably because the something you chose not to do was something you considered to be boring, or just too much effort, right? Most of us consider life to be too short to waste time on dull tasks, but we would do well to consider how much of our lives we still waste on things that really don't matter at all.

A life well lived is a fulfilling life, leaving no room for regrets. It's all about living a life of meaning.

No one on their death bed ever regrets not spending more time at the office!

Finding meaning in your life is finding your own "why" in life. Your why is found in understanding what you value, and what matters most to you.

Fulfilment comes from finding a deep sense of satisfaction in what you do, so it's found in devoting your time and energy to the things that matter most. Of course, there are always going to be aspects of life that don't fill you with a sense of satisfaction, that's life, but with the right attitude, the best can be found in every moment.

If you're not being true to yourself, are you living the life you want to live, or could you be in danger of putting your own hopes and dreams on hold for another day – only to find that you have run out of days?

You already know that staying true to yourself can be challenging in a world that creates pressures from every angle. There's pressure to look a certain way; pressure to be popular; pressure to be (or at least appear to be) successful; pressure to conform, pressure to achieve, accomplish, and get ahead; and perhaps even pressure to earn a certain income... the pressures of modern life, and very often the pressures of others' expectations, can make it difficult to just be yourself, and to stay true to who you want to be. Taking the time to discover what gives you a sense of meaning and purpose in your life is going to help you find greater fulfilment in all you do.

There are no guarantees in life, so making the most of each moment and each day is an essential step in building a life of fulfilment. Life is a balancing act. To find fulfilment, you must balance meaning, purpose, and a plan for the future alongside enjoyment of the simple pleasures that are already yours as you journey towards that future.

"Big Yellow Taxi" is a famous Joni Mitchell song. She sings, "Don't it always seem to go that you don't know what you've got till it's gone". The message in the lyrics is a message for life – choose to appreciate all you *have* from one day to the next, rather than having to lose something before fully appreciating what you *had*.

Chapter 9 – You've Got to Have Faith

Today's world has veered away from the doctrines once firmly anchored in religious teachings, and research points to a notable downturn in the number of churchgoers or those with any religious affiliations. Could there be a

correlation between the decline in church attendance and the escalating trend of moral decline?

The prevailing attitude of instant gratification in society today has developed what feels like an overall slump in moral standards – and these standards are sadly accepted as the 'new normal'. It's normal (if not encouraged) to put yourself and your own needs ahead of others and their needs, and it's normal for differences of opinion to become shouting match battlegrounds with neither side able to respect the other's point of view. What happened to empathy, compassion, respect, and even the common decency to listen to others, let alone openly and fairly discuss differences of opinion?

Observing the state of our world, communities, and even our own families, it's clear that people are increasingly distancing themselves from God's moral compass, opting for self-defined ethics instead.

Individuals seeking wisdom and truth can identify that the current state of affairs is a direct result of the challenge Satan posed to God, as portrayed in the story of Adam and Eve's descent into sin and their subsequent belief that they could not only survive but flourish without adhering to God's laws. Satan's brazen challenge to God's sovereignty is alarmingly apparent in his cunning suggestion that humanity would do better making their own moral judgments.

We need to be steadfast in cultivating good character and high moral values, boldly standing for what is right over what is popular. Christian faith extends beyond a

simple belief; it is an active reliance on God's promises, a light that shines the way to righteousness. This moral compass, with faith as its magnetic north, provides direction in the stormy seas of life.

As those who continue to uphold God's standards, we must persist in seeking wisdom and understanding, as advised in Proverbs 4:7. We need to stand out, but for all the right reasons. We should consider it a privilege to face ridicule for upholding God's laws.

Faith, in Christianity, is the confident conviction of things we hope for and the assurance about what we do not see (Hebrews 11:1). It's more than just acknowledging God's existence, it involves a deep trust in His benevolence, His promises, and His providence.

Faithfulness, one of the fruits of the Spirit (Galatians 5:22), encapsulates the consistent commitment to an assignment despite obstacles or delays, therefore it embodies reliability, dependability, and trustworthiness. To the believer, faithfulness is not merely a quality, but a lifestyle; a commitment to God's word and His commandments.

In an era where moral relativism often reigns supreme, the advantages of adhering to high moral standards, especially those set forth in God's Word, remain a timeless testament to the transformative power of godly living. These standards serve as a guiding compass, steering us through life's complex labyrinth, providing protection against the perils associated with low moral

standards, and unlocking the abundant blessings that stem from obedience to God's commands.

To live by high moral standards is, in essence, choosing to live life to its fullest extent.

To end this chapter, and this book, I leave you with the story of Alexander the Great and his three wishes:

> Alexander was a great Greek king. As a military commander, he was undefeated and the most successful throughout history. On his way home from conquering many lands, he was struck down by an illness. At that moment, his captured territories, powerful army, sharp swords, and wealth suddenly had no meaning to him. He realised that death would soon arrive, and he would be unable to return to his homeland. He told his officers, 'I will soon leave this world. I have three final wishes. I ask you to carry out what I tell you.' His tearful generals agreed.

The Three Wishes

The best doctors should carry my body.

All the wealth I have accumulated (money, gold, precious stones) should be scattered along the procession to the cemetery.

And my body should be covered in a shroud, with only my hands visible, swinging in the wind, palms up, carrying dust.

Surprised by these wishes, one general asked Alexander the Great to explain why he made them. His reply was, 'I want the best doctors to carry my coffin to demonstrate that, in the face of death, even the best doctors in the world have no power to heal. I want the road to be covered with my treasure so that everyone will see that material wealth acquired on earth, stays on earth. I want my hands to swing in the wind, so that people understand that we come to this world empty handed and we leave this world empty handed after the most precious treasure of all is exhausted. That treasure is TIME. The best present you can give to your family and friends, is your time. May God grant you plenty of time and may you have the wisdom to give it away so that you can live, love, and die in peace.'

In choosing to standout for the right reasons in life, you choose to live a life of being and doing your best, and the legacy you leave behind will inspire all who knew you to become the best they can be.

The End